Power-Up

Teams & Tools

for
Process Improvement
&
Problem Solving

William L. Montgomery, PhD
The National Graduate School

Best Wishes,

William L. Montgomery

Power-Up Teams and Tools.

For information contact MCG Publishers, 5 Country Club Lane, Doylestown, PA 18901.

Illustrated by Dale W. Schierholt II, Red Brick Design, Hopewell, NJ 08525

Original printed text ISBN 0-9641124-0-X , printed in the United States. This third National Graduate School edition published March 2003. Electronic files created by Book Masters in Ohio. Printed by Infinity in Haverford, PA

ISBN   0-9641124-3-4

Library of Congress Catalog Card Number 94-96139

They headed in the wrong direction for months.

Instinct told them to head south, but they were in a river and
the south end of that river was a dead end.

First they needed to head north into open waters,
then use their instinct to head south.

They needed a new way of thinking
to save their own lives.

Article on trapped dolphins
New York Times, January 1, 1994

(In February the dolphins followed a lead boat
out of the river and into the Atlantic.)

Dedication

This book is dedicated to Walter A. Shewhart (1891 - 1967), contemporary and fellow quality creator with W. Edwards Deming and Joseph M. Juran. He first envisioned the Plan-Do-Check-Act model that underlies virtually all Quality Efforts and Systems Thinking

Please see the Preface for more information on
Walter Shewhart and the PDCA model.

The Benchmark Award Series
Adding Practical Value To The Body Of Knowledge

The National Graduate School of Quality Management has selected *Power-Up Teams and Tools* for inclusion in its award series because of its established reputation with our students and with the business, public, healthcare, and government sectors. It provides insights to team-based process improvement that come from years of experience and in-depth understanding. The text has a proven ability to accelerate process improvement activities and results for both individuals and organizations. In this new edition, Dr. Montgomery has again constructed a coherent whole of theory, practical tools, examples, and realistic steps.

The National Graduate School has designated this text as required reading in its graduate degree program, and as a recipient of its *Benchmark* Award for practical scholarship.

Robert James Gee
President and Founder
The National Graduate School
of Quality Systems Management

Acknowledgment

All of us are part of a learning and growing environment in which the ideas and experiences of one person or of a team often creates new ideas and approaches for others. There is a sharing and cascading of knowledge that leads to higher levels of effectiveness for everyone.

This book is the result of two decades of such sharing and learning with hundreds of others. I thank my fellow trainers and facilitators of the past and present, as well as hundreds of team members and members of Sytems Councils, and Steering Teams. You have all had a role in shaping the information in this book. We all work to explore, design, and improve business processes of all types. I thank all who have gone before in this effort, and invite others to build on the knowledge presented here.

Many people contributed comments and ideas to this book, but I especially want to thank the following: Tom Hartman of the Shared Services Center in Harrisburg, Diane Ritter in Atlanta, Barbara Katz of Health Interaction Associates in Branford Connecticut, and Michael Brower, a dedicated educator in New England. The faculty of the National Graduate School are wonderfully creative and supportive, and the President of the School, Bob Gee, has been a visionary inspiration. Finally, my special appreciation goes to Loretta, my wife, for her creativity, inspiration, and continual assistance in making this book a reality.

Bill Montgomery

"That's it, Father!", interrupted Pinocchio. "We'll build a great big fire !!"

"Not the chairs!", warned Geppeto.   "What will we sit on?"

"We won't need the chairs," shouted Pinocchio.   "Father, don't you understand? We'll build a big fire and make Monstro sneeze !   When he sneezes, out we go !
Hurry ~~~~ more wood !"

Pinocchio, by Collodi
and Walt Disney

Preface

A Stroll Down....

Over a decade ago, I worked on an evaluation project collecting data on the performance of over five hundred process improvement teams. Ninety different companies were involved in that study. That data reflected the early efforts of company-wide approaches to Total Quality Management, especially in service-oriented companies. Improving business and work processes was, and still is, viewed as critical for customer and employee satisfaction, and for profitability and productivity. Teams were formed and spirits initially ran high.

That early data showed, unfortunately, that about two-thirds of the teams did not complete their intended effort. For those teams, processes remained unchanged and frustration gradually replaced earlier enthusiasm.

Today, success rates can be very high. Teams and individuals can be delighted in their progress and their learning as work processes are streamlined in favor of both the customer and the business. We know now that the tools and techniques teams have been using over the last decade are essentially correct. What has been missing is sufficient understanding in *how to use these tools and techniques effectively*. Teams had thought that the tools could be used in a straight mechanical sense, and that results would be automatic. Any difficulties or inconsistencies with tools was viewed by teams as a sign that the team was failing, or that the tools were simply not working. This view is often expressed by teams even today. *I want to share a very different view with you.* This book was written to show that any difficulties or inconsistencies that occur when using team tools is often the beginning of learning something new and important. The objective is to understand *how* to be effective with the tools and with process improvement.

Specifically, this book explains how to:
- ☐ Achieve the *greatest benefit* from each process improvement and
   problem solving tool.
- ☐ Have more productive and enlightening *communications*.
- ☐ Circumvent the *pitfalls* of each tool.
- ☐ *Construct* each tool, step-by-step.
- ☐ Use each tool, including *when and why*.
- ☐ *Analyze* flow charts.
- ☐ Use the tools to be creative in capturing *customer requirements*.

In addition, this book provides practical insights on:
- ☐ Support areas needed by teams.
- ☐ Process Improvement approaches.
- ☐ Team structure (Process Owner, Leader, etc.) for productive teamwork.

This book has been written for practitioners of process imporvement. We have endeavored to summarize 15 years of team experience into this manual. We had enough course notes, research notes, team meeting notes, and various survey data from both service-oriented companies and manufacturing companies to cover a large desk. Our challenge was to bring this information into one clear summary. We believe that it is essential that all teams involved in process imporvement have this knowledge, and we hope that we have conveyed the information in a clear and useful way for you.

We have designed a certain sequence for presentation of materials and ideas. That sequence, which appears in each tool-oriented chapter, facilitates and enhances use of this manual. You will find, therefore, that each chapter explaining a process imporovement tool has the same basic layout and format. That format is described in Section 7 of the Introduction.

This Preface would not be complete without recognition of three people as the earliest pioneers of quality systems. While approximately a dozen people made significant contributions in the earlier years, the three generally recognized as the pioneers are Drs. Joseph Juran, W. Edwards Deming, and Walter Shewhart. While Shewhart may be less well known, he made lasting contributions. The logo chosen to represent this book - the one found at the top of most pages - is a representation of a model which was first presented by Walter Shewhart in 1939. The model, familiar to many people today, is shown at the right:

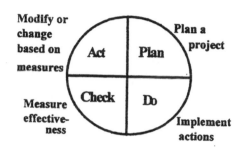

As W. Edwards Deming described in his book *Out of Crisis*, the Shewhart cycle is useful for approaching and guiding projects of any size. It is a model that invites us to conduct continuous improvement by basing our planning on the measurement and evaluation of effectiveness of past performance and activity. This cycle is literally at the foundation of process improvement and problem solving. The application for the Malcolm Baldrige National Quality Award, for example, points out that "learning cycles involve planning, execution of plans, assessment of progress, and revision based on the assessment." Further, The American Society for Quality (ASQ) has long recognized the contributions of Walter Shewhart and named an award in his name, which W. Edwards Deming won in 1955.

In summary, we are at a new threshold in understanding effective teamwork for process improvement. We can use the tools and techniques first introduced by Walter Shewhart and others in ways that allow us to be truly effective. The intent of this book is to help you cross that threshold. Best wishes on your journey as you *Power-Up Teams and Tools.*

Bill Montgomery

Institute a vigorous program of education and retraining !

W. Edwards Deming
Quality Control expert and
advocate;
1900 - 1993

Table of Contents

INTRODUCTION

To find a fault is easy; to do better may be difficult.

Plutarch
Greek biographer
46 - 120 A.D.

Introduction

Teamwork: A Closer Look

The Team Tools in this book include the Pareto chart, radar chart, line graph, supportive action matrix, histogram, customer requirements matrix, and many others. These tools can be effectively used by both teams and individuals to help focus on customer requirements and to improve business processes.

The major purpose of this book is to shed *new and different light* on how we can use these Team Tools to stimulate higher levels of communication, progress, and excitement for any person or team working to improve business processes. In addition, new effective insights are provided on process improvement approaches, on team membership, and more.

NOTES

For the last decade, teams have thought of tools primarily as displays of information. Teams worked to have correct displays. Disagreements over flow chart construction, or interpretation of a Pareto chart, have often been viewed as a sign that the team misused the tools or that these tools simply do not apply to the situation at hand. In fact, the *hidden capability* of some tool may have been right at the edge of being discovered by a team, when frustration caused them to stop!

Uncovering the previously hidden capability of tools is like uncovering a new source of light that illuminates and clarifies new areas of work and communications for teams. Progress will be better, and business process performance will improve both for your customers and for your company. Chapters 1 through 15 provide insights to the construction, potentials, and pitfalls of various important Process Improvement and Problem Solving Tools.

The purpose here, in this Introduction, is to lay groundwork by providing an explanation of vocabulary, concepts, and methods used by successful teams. The idea is to discuss all of this groundwork now in order to enhance understandings of the chapters on Process Improvement tools that follow.

The topics covered in this Introduction are:

    1. Forming a Team is the Easy Part

    2. Process Improvement or Problem Solving - Which is Which?

    3. Tools Are Not Just Tools

    4. Potentials of Tools - What's the Big Deal ?

    5. Pitfalls of Tools - Uh Oh !

    6. Construction of Tools

    7. Structure of this Book

Within these seven sections are suggestions and guidelines based on experience and actual cases. There are also specific points, or axioms. Each point is called an " *Ah ha !* " to reflect the sudden revelation we experience when a useful and significant observation is seen in a new light. Let's begin!

My Ideas and Items to practice at the next team meeting

1. FORMING A TEAM IS THE EASY PART

You have probably heard someone say, "We need to form some teams."   Or,
"I can't wait until teams are formed -- then we will be on our way! "

There is a mental image that forming teams makes the world right - or at least
better. That mental image is about half right.
Our first *"Ah ha ! "* is this:

> *Ah ha !* #1:   Forming teams is not enough to assure high performance.
> Teams need support. Without support, teams are like
> air-filled balloons; they gradually sink to the ground and do not
> move much except when a stray breeze - perhaps some
> organizational event - pushes them about. We need to arrange
> for that support and provide guidance to the team movement.

NOTES

....

....

....

....

....

....

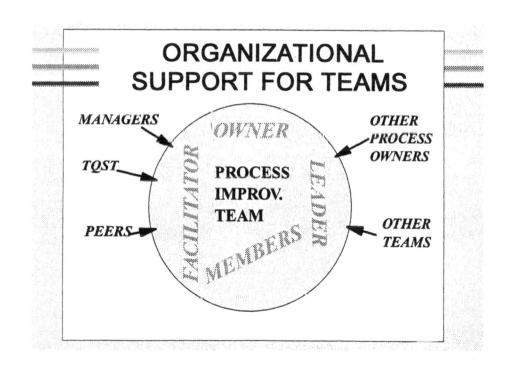

My Ideas and Items to practice at the next team meeting

....

1a WHO GIVES WHAT SUPPORT ?

Here are a few leading questions to ask concerning any team:

☐ Do those who are not on the team understand what the team is working on and why ? This question is especially important for those peers in the same functional work group as the team members, but who are not on the team. Trust can be an issue.

☐ Do the peers agree with the objectives ?

☐ Are others in the organization involved in collecting data, or in gathering information, or in validating flow charts, or in helping to identify customers or customer requirements ?

NOTES

....

....

....

....

....

....

☐ Do the managers of those on the team approve of the time required for team activities ?

☐ Do the managers help remove barriers ?

☐ Do teams share their learning points with other teams?

☐ Is there a Total Quality of Steering Team (TQST) or a similar steering team, that oversees the Process Improvement efforts in the organization, including tracking and supporting teams ?

☐ Has a process owner (also called a process sponsor) been identified ? (See the definition in Section 1b of this Introduction. Also see the Appendix.)

☐ Has the process owner made clear any time frames, measures of success, or goals ?

☐ Does the process owner help remove barriers; review current findings of the team; attend meetings as needed; and meet periodically with the team and team leader ?

My Ideas and Items to practice at the next team meeting

....

....

If the team can answer 'yes' to each of these, it is well supported - it is a lifted balloon that can travel over hurdles and move along. If half of the answers are 'yes', the team is probably in an adequate position. It has some support and can work to achieve the rest.

If few, or none, of these questions are answered affirmatively, the team may be able to recommend improvements and change, but those changes may not be accepted or implemented by others. The last decade is rife with teams that worked arduously in isolation only to be frustrated that their fact-based decisions were not implemented. Remember, and work on, *Ah ha ! #1. Chapters 1 through15 cover the effective use of Process Improvement tools and will greatly help with the communication that is needed to be able to answer each of these questions 'yes'.*

1b PROCESS OWNER/SPONSOR

The Appendix show the roles, criteria for selection, and guidelines concerning four types of process improvement participants: process owner, team leader, team member, and facilitator. Let's look especially at the role of the process owner, also called the process sponsor.

After a few years of analyzing the success and failure factors of hundreds of teams, we have arrived at the second *Ah ha !* :

> *Ah ha ! #2:*   Identify a process owner/sponsor as soon as possible. Do not work too long on improving a process without a process owner/sponsor.

Why ? Because the team needs someone who can say, " I understand the proposed change and I approve. We will implement the change." That is the role of the process owner/sponsor. Without a process owner, teams search for approval and can be like Diogenes, of ancient Greece who walked for years in the dark with a lantern searching for an honest man.

Suppose that a team starts without a process owner/sponsor being identified. Certainly this can happen, because the process to be addressed is not clearly

My Ideas and Items to practice at the next team meeting

identified, or the process may be complex, or there simply is not an understanding yet of which one of several people would best be the process owner/sponsor. The common question is: Can the team be effective in having the process owner/sponsor join them later, rather than at the very beginning of the effort ? The answer is most definitely 'yes', as long as a process owner/sponsor is eventually aligned with the team. Just remember, *Ah ha !* #2 is virtually a rule !

Here are other commonly asked questions and the answers we have found to be effective:

☐ Can the process owner/sponsor also be the team leader ?
> Yes, but this is generally not as effective as having a process owner/ sponsor *and* a team leader. Having two people allows sharing of ideas and more effective planning for meetings and approaches. In addition, the team facilitator can assist in the sharing of ideas between the process owner and the team leader. He or she can be a coach, advisor, and sounding board.

☐ Must the process owner/sponsor understand the business process thoroughly?
> No, but they should consider learning the process fully with the team. Understanding the flow charts, the customers, customer requirements, and the like, is crucial.

☐ Can more than one person be the process owner/sponsor ?
> Yes, but if at all possible, have only one person making decisions on the changes that will be implemented. Processes that cut across functional or organizational boundaries will be the most difficult ones in which to have a single process owner/sponsor. If a few people can work together and act as one unified body in their decision making and interactions with the team, that is certainly the most effective and advantageous arrangement.

☐ Can the process owner/sponsor decide unilaterally to make changes in the process ?
> No. Process owners/sponsors need to discuss the proposed changes with stakeholders inside and outside of the process. They need to discuss their plans with other process owners/sponsors if other processes are affected.

My Ideas and Items to practice at the next team meeting

NOTES

1c HOW TO GET SUPPORT FOR GETTING SUPPORT

Here we are, on a team. We now know that *Ah ha !* #1 and #2 are saying:

     ' *Get support* ' and ' *Have a process owner/sponsor* '

Fine. But if we don't have a process owner/sponsor, how do we proceed ? How do we communicate the scope of the business process, the impact that improving it can have, the importance of having a process owner/sponsor, and the logical person for that position?   How do we communicate these things?

The beauty of the tools is that they are for more than displaying data - that is where their potential comes into play. They help us *communicate* within the team and with others. The Process Improvement and Problem Solving Tools will support the team in finding support. For example, show your column flow chart to others, as discussed in Chapter 2. Discuss the problems and ask for help in identifying a process owner. Likewise, show the intermediate-level flow chart, the customer requirements matrix, and data displays on current performance. The TQM Tools facilitate our communication and assist in gaining support.

NOTES

2. PROCESS IMPROVEMENT OR PROBLEM SOLVING - WHICH IS WHICH ?

The story is probably familiar to most quality facilitators and team members:

> Some business process is causing difficulty for employees and for customers. A team is formed to improve and change procedures, or the material used, or some aspect of how the job is conducted. That is their goal.

> But there is a dilemma. Is this a Process Improvement activity or a Problem Solving activity ? How should the team approach it ? What is the scope of the effort ?

A standard question asked when starting teams is: "Will these be Process Improvement Teams, or Problem Solving teams?" The answer may not be obvious because people are not sure how to begin. Some companies have teams for both,

My Ideas and Items to practice at the next team meeting

while others have only Process Improvement teams but use a Process Improvement methodology that contain a set of Problem Solving steps.

Is there a difference between Process Improvement and Problem Solving, and does it matter ?

There is a difference, but it is not always easy to tell which is which. There are, however, distinguishing characteristics that begin with the difference between a process and a problem.

A PROCESS

☐ A process can be visualized and drawn as a flow of activities, starting with information or raw materials coming into some initial activity that begins to transform that input.

☐ A process provides, as output, a product or a service that is the result of converting the input. We refer to this conversion when we say that a process 'adds value'.

☐ A process may involve work activities spanning different departments.

☐ A process may be complex or simple.

☐ A process usually has multiple problems or opportunities for improvement. The team works to locate those problems or opportunities and to select one to address first.

A PROBLEM

☐ A problem means a standard or a customer requirement is not being met.

☐ A problem may be a malfunction, or it may be a design flaw.

☐ A problem is a specific situation. It cannot be drawn as a flow of activities. If a flow is drawn, the flow is of a process. Inside of that flow may lie a faulty situation -- that is, a problem.

My Ideas and Items to practice at the next team meeting

NOTES

2a SO WHAT'S THE PROBLEM?

The distinction between 'process' and 'problem' probably seems clear enough in concept. There is no similarity, except that *processes can have problems.*

Why, then, is there a confusion on whether a team is working on Process Improvement or Problem Solving ?

Let's take a few examples. Decide whether each one is a Process Improvement (PI) or a Problem Solving (PS) activity for a team. Use the distinguishing characteristics above to guide your decision. Answers are on the next page.

1. A work group within the shipping department has the task of printing labels that are then placed on custom-made electronic devices sold to customers. The computer printer often jams when plastic coated paper is fed through it, yet that type of paper is needed for labels because it is durable. The work group meets to improve the situation.

    Circle one: PI   or   PS

2. In a hospital, doctors write prescriptions which then go to nurses and then to the hospital pharmacy. In one particular hospital, prescriptions are often hours late reaching hospital patients, and the staff decides to meet to correct the situation.

    Circle one: PI   or   PS

3. In a particular publishing company, cycle time in processing and delivering customer orders is two days longer than that of the competition.

    Circle one: PI   or   PS

NOTES

My Ideas and Items to practice at the next team meeting

4. In a company that assembles small parts into computer work stations, lack of adequate record size in the customer order file causes rejects that in turn cause delivery delays in ten percent of the orders.

       Circle one: PI   or   PS

5. Data collected by an office work group shows that customer billing is incorrect 30% of the time because addresses are incorrect.

       Circle one: PI   or   PS

NOTES

....

....

....

....

....

....

....

My Ideas and Items to practice at the next team meeting

....

....

SUGGESTED ANSWERS TO EACH OF THE EXAMPLES ABOVE:

1. This is a problem to be solved. It is a single situation: The printer jams. A type of label that satisfies the computer printer and the shipping department must be found. Alternatively, a new approach to labeling may be possible.

2. This is a process to be improved. There is a flow of information and materials, and there must be some time-eaters in that flow.

3. This is a process to be improved. The flow of handling customer orders needs to be streamlined.

4. This is a problem to be solved. Note that there is an order process, but a major problem within it has been identified.

5. Probably a process to be improved. Incorrect addresses are an issue, but the process that creates those addresses has some difficulty that has not yet been identified.

From the above we can see that 'processes' and 'problems' are very different, but *there is* a relationship between Process Improvement and Problem Solving! First, let's recognize the distinction between a *problem* and an *opportunity*, then we can explore that relationship :

Problem - standards are not being met. Customers may be complaining.

Opportunity - standards are being met. Customers are not complaining, but we can make an improvement.

Now we can state the relationship between Process Improvement and Problem Solving. In particular, Problem Solving is one way of achieving Process Improvement.

Process Improvement happens In two ways:

1. Identify and correct problems in the process.

2. Take advantage of an opportunity in the process.

My Ideas and Items to practice at the next team meeting

In other words, Process Improvement involves finding a specific area of the process flow which has a problem or an opportunity, and changing that area of the process. That specific area may be large or small. It may be one step in the process flow, or an interconnected set of steps. It may be one data base, or one piece of equipment, or it may even be a set of reference books used in the process, or a policy that is used in the making of decisions. Likewise, the improvement may be a small change, in which case we tend to say:

> ' We just completed a small but significant incremental
> improvement in our work flow! '

Or, the improvement may involve changing a considerable portion of the overall flow, in which case we tend to say:

> ' We redesigned the process. It is very different from what we
> had before. It has been reengineered! '

2b A METHOD TO OUR MADNESS ?

Process Improvement teams need a methodology - a set of steps - to guide them. *A generalized methodology is shown below.* This methodology has been successfully used by hundreds of teams and individuals. It is shown not only as an example of a successful approach, but also as a generic or generalized approach. There are others that work well, but all methods are roughly the same because there are certain steps that any Process Improvement team must consider. The primary issue here is not **what** steps to use as a guide, but rather **how** to travel through those steps. This leads us to the next *Ah ha !*

Ah ha ! #3: Having a methodology to guide Process Improvement or Problem Solving teams is important, but more important is **how** the team journeys through that method. That is why using the tools to their fullest potential is important - the tools help teams walk through any methodology efficiently and effectively.

NOTES

My Ideas and Items to practice at the next team meeting

The methodology shown below is called the Dynamic Process Improvement Method (DPI Method). The term 'dynamic' is important here because it conveys the nature of this method and the philosophy in constructively using it. The idea is to construct and learn at one stage, move on, and move back to a previous stage as needed. A dynamic flow is the most effective way to proceed. The term 'stage' likewise was selected to convey this effective flow, as discussed later.

A brief background on the DPI Method may be helpful:

○ It was developed by studying *natural* stages that teams use effectively in describing and streamlining work flows.

○ It is *generalized*, or 'generic', in the sense that it describes the major stages that a team utilizes. Other methods generally follow or fit into these major stages. Learning these stages is a grounding for understanding virtually any process improvement method.

○ It is *simple* to use and understand.

○ It is *dynamic*. We learn and take action at a stage, then move on, knowing that we may need to return to a previous stage. *Returning is effective.*

NOTES

....

....

....

....

....

....

My Ideas and Items to practice at the next team meeting

....

Dynamic Process Improvement Method (DPI Method)

A Generalized Method for Improving Processes

| Stage 1 | Scope | What process are we, the team, really working on? What are the boundaries? Who is the process owner? Who would be the appropriate team members, as far we can tell right now? |

| Stage 2 | Flow | Describe the flow of the process with a Column Flow Chart (Chapter 2) and perhaps a Basic Flow Chart (Chapter 3). Identify inefficiencies and bottle necks. Identify key data collection points. |

| Stage 3 | Customer/ Supplier | Determine the customer requirements in measurable ways. Use a Customer Requirements Matrix. Explain *your* process requirements to your supplier(s). |

| Stage 4 | Issues | Collect, display, and analyze data. Based on this and on discoveries from the first three stages, make a list of *problems* or *opportunities*. This list is called the 'Issues' list. Select one Issue to address using a Decision Matrix or the like. |

| Stage 5 | Cause | Find the root cause of the Issue. |

| Stage 6 | Solution | Identify and implement a solution that will reduce or eliminate the root cause and thereby reduce or remove the Issue. Plan for a next improvement in the process. |

NOTES

....

....

....

....

....

....

My Ideas and Items to practice at the next team meeting

....

....

These six items are called 'stages', rather than 'steps', for a very good reason. The word 'steps' implies to most of us that there is a continual progression and no looking back. In fact, in many team efforts we have seen, to go back is taken as a sign of moderate failure. To go back suggests that somehow the work was not properly done the 'first time through'. Well, the Shewhart Cycle of 'Plan, Do, Check, and Act' does *not* say 'do it right the first time'. Instead the whole approach is to '**plan** to do it right the first time'. Going back to a previous step is perfectly appropriate when it enhances our going forward. As a team, we do what we can at one step and move forward. We may need to go back.

Our experience with teams is that cycling back is *not only* effective, but good management of a learning cycle and of clarity of purpose. Data at one step often suggests that the team needs to return to a previous step. In fact, we usually find that after drawing a flow of a process at Stage 2, a team has better insight on who the subprocess owners and team members need to be. The team may need to return to Stage 1 to consider some modification in team membership or roles. This is an efficacious way to proceed and is, in fact, recommended. The term 'stage', therefore, has been selected to reflect the philosophy that each is simply a place to be. They are not irreversible steps, as in a cookbook or instructions for assembling a bicycle. You can go back.

Now here is another point that may reduce the confusion between Process Improvement and Problem Solving: *The last three stages of the DPI Method are actually a Problem Solving Method.* Is that true for most Process Improvement Methods? *Yes*! If the Process Improvement Method is one that is written to select a problem or opportunity in the process and to correct it, then the last stages of that method will be Problem Solving in nature. This leads us to *Ah ha !* #4:

> *Ah ha !* #4 A Process Improvement Methodology will usually have within it the steps, stages, or activities for solving a problem. Often those can be extracted and used separately as a Problem Solving set of steps.

Let's take a look at this Problem Solving nature of Stages 4, 5, and 6 above. Each of the Stages in the DPI Method actually have more detailed activities within them that can guide a team. Those activities are listed below for Stages 4, 5, and 6:

My Ideas and Items to practice at the next team meeting

NOTES

DETAILED ACTIVITIES FOR STAGES 4, 5, AND 6

Stage 4   Issues

☐ Collect more internal and external data on the process as needed.
☐ Identify problems or opportunities from previous stages and previous data.
☐ Make a list of all Issues (both Problems and Opportunities).
☐ Select one Issue to address.
☐ Discuss the results with others who use, or are involved with, the process.

Stage 5   Cause

☐ Identify candidates for the primary, or root, cause(s) of the Issue.
☐ Verify that the candidate root cause is actually a root cause via data.
☐ Document that root cause.

Stage 6   Solution

☐ Generate possible solutions to correct the root cause.
☐ Select one to implement first.
☐ Test the solution, as needed.
☐ Plan for contingencies, as needed.
☐ Implement the solution.
☐ Plan for continuous improvement by approaching the next Issue.

These three stages provide a basis for a solid Problem Solving method.

My Ideas and Items to practice at the next team meeting

....

....

2c PROCESS MANAGEMENT, YOU SAY ?

Yes, there is yet another concept around process change that adds to our vocabulary. The term 'Process Management' can have two basic meanings. It can mean:

1. Process Improvement. Exactly the same concept, but different words. An example is: ' We are a Process Management Team - we have a process owner, we are collecting data, drawing flow charts, and talking to customers in order to find the primary difficulty in this process and the root cause of it so we can recommend and implement a solution .' You can see this use of Process Management on an excellent video by Video Arts called 'The Customer is Always Dwight.'

or

2. Oversight of several Process Improvement Teams. An example is: 'We are a Process Management Group that supports four Process Improvement Teams by helping to remove barriers. Most of us in the group are process owners for the processes those teams are addressing.

3. TOOLS ARE NOT JUST TOOLS

The word itself - *tools* - is an understatement for Quality Systems Managment. Various dictionaries define a tool as:

An instrument used in the creative arts to facilitate manual operations.

Each of these: A Pareto diagram, histogram, radar chart, run chart, pie chart, decision matrix, and the others, are more than just *tools* that follow that definition. True, when Process Improvement efforts first began as a company-wide initiative, we tended to regard team tools as mechanical means to achieve some specific mechanical end or result, such as displaying data, or displaying options. Today we understand much more.

My Ideas and Items to practice at the next team meeting

NOTES

When used to their full potential, TQM tools are also:

- Vehicles to uncover patterns, inconsistencies, difficulties, successes, and possibilities.
- Vessels that carry ideas and information.
- Visual displays of team findings, constructions, and results.

In short, the *hidden power of tools* is their ability to greatly facilitate communications.

NOTES

....

....

....

....

....

....

....

Within Chapters 1 through 15 that follow, is guidance in several areas, including these three:

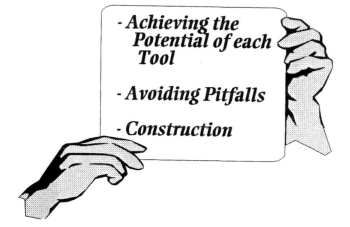

- *Achieving the Potential of each Tool*

- *Avoiding Pitfalls*

- *Construction*

The next three sections below, Sections 4, 5, and 6, provide an introduction to each of these areas.

My Ideas and Items to practice at the next team meeting

....

....

4. POTENTIALS OF TOOLS -
WHAT'S THE BIG DEAL

Each chapter describing a tool has a section entitled 'Achieving Potentials.' The tips, hints, and suggestions in each chapter are the result of years of working and experimenting. We have found that those teams that have worked to uncover the hidden power of tools will experience:

☐ New insights to the business process being explored for improvement, or the problem being addressed.

☐ New insights to their own team dynamics.

☐ Graphical displays showing customer and supplier interactions.

☐ Guidance from the tools on
- next steps
- effective team membership
- opportunity areas
- logical approaches
- focus
- clarity

☐ Consensus and support among team members because data and ideas are focused and visible.

☐ Support from others outside of the team because the information from the tools is clear and pertinent to them.

NOTES

The next figure illustrates the relative potential of several Tools on Team effectiveness, as described above. The tools are also shown according to relative difficulty. The positions in this figure vary from team to team and from one circumstance to another, but we have found this chart to be essentially correct.

My Ideas and Items to practice at the next team meeting

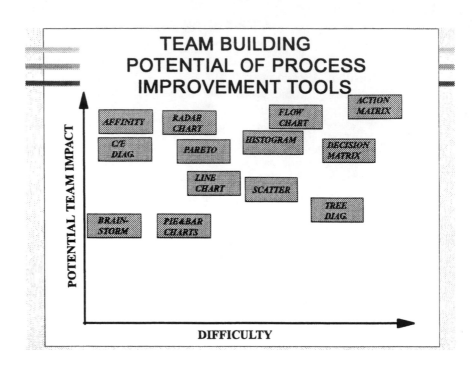

NOTES

....

....

....

....

....

....

5. PITFALLS OF THE TOOLS -
UH OH !

Each chapter here that describes a tool provides guidance on avoiding pitfalls. Certainly no team wants to 'fall into a pit', or become 'bogged down', or 'get stuck' when using the tools. But it happens. When a team is 'in a pit', full potential is difficult. Frustration can occur. The pit can become deeper.

To achieve the fullest potential, therefore, teams must not only work on the 'Achieving Potential' guidelines in each chapter, they must also work on the 'Avoiding Pitfalls' guidelines.

I am reminded of the time I saw sheep in New Zealand grazing on a hillside and walking slowly around as they ate. Not one of them ever looked up to see, or even to consider, where it was going. They all wandered about together with their heads

My Ideas and Items to practice at the next team meeting

....

....

down, completely engrossed in the task of eating. Teams can do that, too. With all good intentions, teams often gather data, construct charts, and discuss items - but forget to look around and to adjust their journey.

Our advice, learned from years of helping teams be successful in their efforts, is to plan not only for the successes and the potentials, but plan for avoiding the pitfalls as well. Discuss the pitfalls ahead of time. Discuss the ones that are presented in each chapter. See if they apply to your work. Could they happen? What can be done to avoid them. Consider the avoidance steps suggested with each tool.

6. CONSTRUCTION OF TOOLS

Each chapter that is dedicated to a tool provides detailed steps for construction. In addition, there is a **'Quick View'** of construction on a single page. The construction steps also provide tips and hints on expanded approaches and on effective ways to gain extra insights through attention to certain details.

7. STRUCTURE OF THIS BOOK

To facilitate using this manual, each chapter describing a tool has the same basic sequence:

First -   A description of basic reasons or *motivations* teams
           have for using, or needing, the particular tool.

Second -   A summary description of (1) *What* the tool provides,
           (2) *Why* use it, and (3) *When* to use it.

Third -   A *'Quick View'* on how to construct and use the
           tool.

Fourth -   A description of the *Potentials* that can be achieved
           with each tool, followed by a description of the
           Pitfalls that teams encounter, and how to avoid
           them.

My Ideas and Items to practice at the next team meeting

Fifth -   A step-by-step description of how to *construct* each tool.

Sixth -   *Examples* throughout each chapter to display the concepts.

Chapter 1 describes an Affinity Diagram and how to use it effectively. It is a very effective tool for changing chaotic meetings into productive ones.

Chapters 2 and 3 are dedicated to Flow Charts. Each of those two chapters have an additional page that describes types of flow charts.

Chapter 4 presents Tools for Analyzing Flow Charts. This is, in essence, an advanced concept for teams that can greatly improve flow of business processes.

Chapter 5 describes a Customer Requirements Matrix, which is an excellent way to understand and to capture customer needs.

Chapter 6 provides guidelines on what data display tools to use in different situations.

Chapters 7, 8, and 9 describe Pie, Bar and Line charts, respectively.

Chapters 10 and 11 describe Pareto charts and Histograms, respectively.

Chapter 12 explains the effective use of a Radar Chart in various creative situations.

Chapter 13 shows how to use a Cause and Effect Diagram as a major step to uncovering root causes of problems.

Chapter 14 explains the Decision Matrix which greatly aids in achieving consensus, while Chapter 15 explains the use of a Supportive Action Matrix, which facilitates team action and projects.

The Appendix provides guidelines, insights and useful planning sheets and tracking sheets - all for use by teams that want effective meetings.

Finally, the **Glossary** provides a description of key terms and ideas in team work, problem solving, and process improvement.   **Read it!   Let's get started !**

My Ideas and Items to practice at the next team meeting

NOTES

Geese, flying in a 'V' formation, add 70 percent flying range to the distance any single bird can fly alone.

The best way to get a good idea is to get a lot of ideas.

Linus Pauling
Chemist
Nobel Prize for Chemistry 1954
Nobel Prize for Peace 1963

SITUATION:

Team Members Say -

"We all have so many ideas. I'm concerned that we will never get off the ground!"

"I agree! This project has so many possibilities that I'm confused!"

"And if one person decides how to proceed, and does, the rest of our ideas may not be used."

"There must be a better way!"

SOLUTION:

Affinity Diagram

I have never in my life learned anything from anyone
who agreed with me.
--Dudley Field Malone

Affinity Diagram

What Is It:

A collection of note cards into vertical groupings. Header cards at the top of each vertical column describe the theme of each grouping.

Why Use It:

- To identify the *Elements of Success* for any organizational goals or any project
- To feel a sense of *progress* when an otherwise confusing meeting might result
- To gain the true *participation* of each team member in identifying key areas of a project
- To gather ideas and to use *all of them* in establishing direction
- To *automatically document* and categorize all ideas for action

When:

- During any meeting where multiple ideas are overflowing
- Whenever confusion exists on how to begin and what to do
- At the early stages of a project to identify the functional areas to address
- During identification of what to do in order to achieve a corporate mission or vision
- In place of brainstorming a list of actions if that list will give little guidance on key areas

He that complies against his will is of his own opinion still.
--Samuel Butler

<u>*QUICK VIEW*</u>

<u>*AFFINITY DIAGRAM*</u>

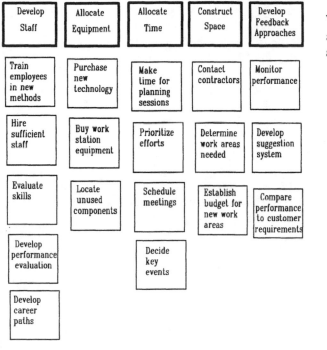

**What are all the
activities needed to
achieve our project**

<u>*NOTES*</u>

1. Write the issue statement clearly.
   (For example, ' What are all the activities needed to achieve -- ')
2. Each person uses 3 to 5 words on each note card.
3. Use a verb on each note card.
4. Target for 5 to 10 note cards per person.
5. Organize the note cards into vertical categories.
   (Doing this in silence is often beneficial.)
6. Place a 'header' card at the top of each vertical category.
7. The header cards describe the key areas for success of the
   project.
8. The Affinity Diagram can be used for small projects or large,
   and is effective in beginning corporate strategic planning.

My Ideas and Items to practice at the next team meeting

Achieve these Potentials

<u>*NOTES*</u>

POTENTIALS	ACHIEVING POTENTIALS
Confusing meetings are converted to productive ones	The Affinity diagram is absolutely superb at allowing participants in any meeting to arrange logic and order out of a chaos of ideas. This benefit of order out of chaos is achieved simply by following the construction guidelines later in this chapter. We often find, however, that team members are at first hesitant to use this tool - until they have tried it once! Ideas fall into place and people feel heard.
New direction setting is shared and understood	Bringing together the leadership of an organization, or of a project, to use the Affinity Diagram leads to identification of key functional areas that can take the organization to a new level. We find the Affinity to be approximately 80 percent complete with ideas the first time it is generated by the team. Additional ideas are gained as the diagram is shared with others in the organization, and as actions begin - which uncovers the need for other items or actions.
Elements of success are identified and clear	The team using the Affinity needs to be the one in charge of the project. The tool can be used for small projects or large. It can be used well, for example, in strategic planning. Use a verb on each note card in order to begin a proactive approach through the tool. The resultant headers at the top of each vertical category will be proactive and will capture the key functional areas that need to be addressed in order to achieve the vision or the goal.
Automatic documentation	The ideas of each person will be written and organized into the whole. The structure and the individual ideas will be visible. The chart can be saved as it is, or it can be transcribed to a smaller sheet for inclusion in the meeting notes.

My Ideas and Items to practice at the next team meeting

POTENTIALS	ACHIEVING POTENTIALS
No idea is lost	By each person writing their action oriented ideas on note cards, that are then sorted into categories, no idea will be lost, and every idea contributes to the whole. Do not discard a note card because it appears to be a duplicate of someone else's until both people have been asked about the meaning or their card. Most often, the words may be the same, but the intention is different. Change the words as needed and save both cards. If the intention is in fact the same for both people, then the two cards can be combined, with their approval.
Everyone participates	Contributions from all individuals are captured on the note cards. Not only is everyone on the team participating in generating the cards, each person then participates in arranging the cards into similar categories. Those cards that have a common purpose (an 'affinity' for each other) are grouped together. Each person is involved in both generating the ideas, and in forming the structure of those ideas that will activate the project.

Achieve these Potentials

NOTES

....

....

....

....

....

....

....

My Ideas and Items to practice at the next team meeting

Learn from these Pitfalls

NOTES

....

....

....

....

....

....

....

PITFALLS	AVOIDING PITFALLS
Confusion on the types of ideas to generate	Be certain that the issue statement is clear. This can often be accomplished by first asking what the team wants to accomplish. Be certain that the goal is clear. Write it for everyone on the team to see. The issue statement can usually be written as 'What are all the actions we need to take to achieve this goal ?' If the goal is more in the form of a vision, the issue statement can be 'What are all of the characteristics and activities that need to be achieved for us to fit this vision ?'
Statements on the note cards that are unclear	The first general guideline is to be certain that verbs are being used. Generally in our projects we want to become proactive rather than reactive. This requires the use of verbs in the Affinity, such as 'establish --, develop --, survey --'. Starting with 'what is --' ,or with 'would we --' generally causes a problem because there is no clear direction. Also, use three to five words, as a guide. Long sentences can create confusion at this point.
Long vertical groupings with perhaps 20 cards in one group	More than around ten cards in a column is a signal that there are multiple ideas or themes within that grouping. Close inspection will often reveal that the long column of cards can be split into two or three columns, each of which is a single theme. Further, the new columns, each with its own header, can often be placed under one 'super header'.
A few people not participating in the grouping of the cards into vertical columns	We have found two approaches that help to assure participation. First, invite the team to sort the cards in silence! While at first they may think it odd, they soon enjoy the ability to place cards wherever they want - and they feel free to participate. Second, point out that the position of each card is the responsibility of each person - everyone is responsible for each card. If someone does not like the placement of a card into a particular grouping, they move it. If someone moves it back, then duplicate that card and

My Ideas and Items to practice at the next team meeting

....

....

PITFALLS	AVOIDING PITFALLS
	place it in both vertical groupings. The team will probably find later that the card has a somewhat different meaning in each grouping.
Important actions or ideas are missing, but the team does not realize it	The objective is to have an Affinity Diagram that captures all of the key functional areas that need to be addressed to achieve the goal or the vision. While the first effort of the team may not be complete, there are ways to assure completeness of key areas.

First, regard the Affinity Diagram as a living document. Take it to others in the organization. Show them what you are doing and ask for their ideas. Ask what might be missing. Second, remember that note cards can be added to the Affinity Diagram at any time. If new ideas are uncovered at a meeting, add them. Perhaps new groupings will result.

We have found that effective deployment of plans results more from a dynamic movement of being willing to go back to add and modify, than from attempting to retain a purely forward, step-by-step approach.

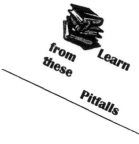

Learn from these Pitfalls

NOTES

My Ideas and Items to practice at the next team meeting

What are all the characteristcs and items we must create or develop to be the best service provider in our community ?

Understand customer needs	Understand our competition	Arrange resources		Train in new approaches	
Survey potential clients	Visit competit. locations	Develop new space		Develop technical skills	Develop people skills
Gather demog raphics	Bench- mark outside	Purchase equip- ment		Bring in trainer on equipment	Evaluate current skills
Hold focus grp discussions	Ask cust- omers about compet.	Hire people for R.A. unit		Arrange for coop. training	Gain support from superv.
Inteview past customers		Arrange financial support			Develop ongoing training

HOW TO CONSTRUCT AN AFFINITY DIAGRAM

1. Begin by seeing the need for, or even the possibility for, an Affinity diagram. If many ideas exist in the meeting, or if the team wants to identify the major areas to address in order to achieve a project or even a strategic plan, the Affinity diagram is a superb tool.

> ☑ *Tip: Next time you are in a meeting that appears to be a bit chaotic, consider using the Affinity Diagram. Simply say, " I have an idea. Let's write our ideas on note cards. This is a tool I have learned that I think will work well here. Let's try it."*

My Ideas and Items to practice at the next team meeting

2. Give each person note cards. The self-sticking type of note cards, such as Post-It™ Notes by 3M, work well.

3. Give each person a marker. While markers are optional, they provide the advantage of being able to see each person's notes and ideas when the cards are placed on the wall or on an easel. It is difficult to read notes from three or more feet away when pencil is used.

> ☑ *Tip: Our minds are stimulated by colors, smells, and sounds. Giving the team members five or six different colored markers adds interest to the meeting and may help spark ideas.*

4. Be certain that the objective of the overall project is clear. What is the goal? What is the Vision?

> ☑ *Tip: Write, or at least outline, the objective so all on the team can see it.*

5. Write the Issue Statement for the Affinity Diagram. The Issue Statement asks a question. Basically it is asking 'What are all the items we need to address in order to achieve our goals (vision, mission, objectives)?' A more comprehensive form of an Issue Statement is as follows:

> ' What are all the elements, characteristics, items, and programs that we need to develop or achieve in order to achieve our goals? '

6. Provide the following instructions to the team before they begin writing their ideas and suggestions:
   a. Three to five words per note card. (Longer wording can be confusing to read at this point. But remember 3 -5 words is a guide. If someone needs seven words, that is fine. We want their ideas.)

   b. Use a verb to start each note. Verbs provide action and explain the direction that is being recommended. For example, 'training' by itself provides no information on what direction to take 'training'; more, less, development, or delivery. We can not tell. But if the note says 'increase' or 'develop', or 'support', or 'assess', then we understand the basic intent and the action that is required.

   c. Each person can be expected to generate five to ten notes, each with one idea or suggestion on it.

My Ideas and Items to practice at the next team meeting

NOTES

NOTES

....

....

....

....

....

....

d. They do not need to be concerned with duplication of ideas at this time. Everyone participates and generates all the ideas they can. Open discussion is encouraged as the cards are generated. Questioning each other's ideas, however, is not generally productive. Support each other in generating as many ideas as possible. Duplicates will be handled later.

> ☑   *Tip: Usually ideas that appear to be duplicates really are not. The words may be the same, but the detailed intentions may not be the same, so both cards are valuable.*

e. Now the team members write. Twenty to thirty minutes is usually sufficient.

7. The note cards are now placed on a large surface. Two easel sheets taped together and taped on the wall serves as a good background for the self-sticking note cards. Ask the team to simply place the cards on the surface in a random order.

8. Ask the team members to discuss the cards. Now is their chance to understand what others have written, and to look for needed but missing items.

9. Now ask the team to sort the cards into vertical groups, with each group representing a single theme.

> ☑   *Tip: Ask them to be as 'clean' within each column as possible, having only one theme in a column and not a mixture of cards that appear to be one theme but are not.*

10. Suggest that they do the sorting in silence! This may surprise them, but it has the advantage of allowing each person to place each card where they believe it belongs.

> ☑   *Tip: If a silent debate arises over having a single card in two different columns, duplicate the card.*

11. After the columns are generated, the team will place a header card at the top of each column. That card captures the theme of the vertical grouping. These header cards are the Elements of Success for the project.

12. The team has not only identified the functional areas, or elements, for achieving the project, they have automatically documented their joint ideas and opinions.

My Ideas and Items to practice at the next team meeting

....

....

We know what we are, but know not what we may be.

William Shakespeare

If we do not change the direction of this ship, it will end up where it is heading !

Author Unknown

SITUATION:

Team Members Say -

❝We seem to be talking about different parts of this process.❞

❝I need a picture to understand what we are dealing with.❞

❝Let's draw a simple flow - one that is high level.❞

❝Alright. I need to somehow understand what departments are involved and how they work.❞

SOLUTION:

Column Flow Chart

Action may not always bring happiness; but there is no happiness without action.
--Benjamin Disraeli

FLOW CHARTS ARE KEY TOOLS

THEY MAKE OUR PROCESS VISIBLE

<u>TYPES OF FLOW CHARTS</u>

- **MACRO FLOW CHART-**

  Shows the flow of a process at high level.   Generally no decision boxes; only activities.

  P H A R M A C Y   O R D E R   P R O C E S S

  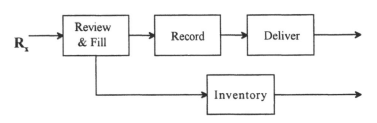

- **COLUMN FLOW CHART-**

  A high level or macro flow chart, in which the activities are placed in columns that represent the organization (departments, groups, people) involved.

- **BASIC (INTERMEDIATE-LEVEL) FLOW CHART-**

  Shows the details within the high level activities of a macro flow chart. Decision boxes are present. Fairly detailed steps shown.

- **MICRO FLOW CHART-**

  Shows every movement involved in an activity or decision. Used especially in 'time-and-motion' studies and in very detailed analysis.

My Ideas and Items to practice at the next team meeting

Column Flow Chart

What Is It:

A high level or macro flow chart of a process in which the activities are placed in columns that represent the organizations involved.

Why Use It:

- To have a clear and simple *picture* of your process
- To identify people, *organizations* , or functional areas involved
- To clarify *boundaries*
- To specify activities and specify flow among those *activities*
- To identify data collection *points*
- To form a *document* of the process that changes as the process is improved

When:

- Multiple departments, or work groups, are involved
- Clarification of the process is needed easily and quickly
- An Intermediate-Level Flow Chart will be constructed, but a common basis is needed first

COLUMN FLOW CHART

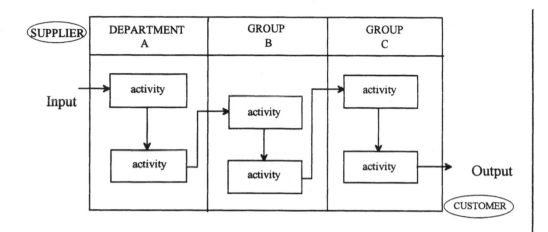

NOTES

....

....

....

....

....

....

....

1. Name the process.

2. State purpose of process.

3. Determine output and customer.

4. Determine input and supplier.

5. Determine organizations or people involved.

6. Determine activities in each column.

7. Draw the connecting flow arrows among the activities.

My Ideas and Items to practice at the next team meeting

....

....

Achieve these Potentials

NOTES

POTENTIALS	ACHIEVING POTENTIALS
A Living Document	The column flow chart shows the *current* flow and activities of the process being explored for improvement. But it can be a *living* document by using it to record changes, improvements, and solutions to problems. Show measurement points and types of data at those points. Show names of people who do the activities. Attach meeting notes and action plans to a large version of the column flow chart that is on the meeting room wall - outside, where everyone can see it. *Trust and support from peers increases !*
Identifies Subprocesses and Subprocess Owners (See the Appendix for the description and role of a "Process Owner")	Within a vertical column, all groups of activities that are linked together make a subprocess. This means that each column is a subprocess, or more. The head of each column identifies the owner for the subprocesses in that column and organization. For example, a "Finance" heading means that someone in the Finance group - usually the head of the group - is the subprocess owner. *Functions are clearer.*
	Finance Subprocess Subprocesses
Identifies Team Members	The most effective team, in general, has the subprocess owners on it, or empowered representatives. The original layout of the team, therefore, may change somewhat from the original group. This is natural and positive once the column flow chart shows what organizations are involved.
Clarifies the Process being Explored	Perhaps for the first time, the process is visible in a clear, simple way and the organizations and people involved can see the work being done and how it is done.
Shows Relationship between Internal Customers and Internal Suppliers	The output of a subprocess is the input to some other sub-process. This is a hand-off between an internal supplier and an internal customer. These hand-offs make the links in a chain that provide the output to the customer outside the overall process. The needs of internal customers must be met to satisfy the external customer.

My Ideas and Items to practice at the next team meeting

PITFALLS	AVOIDING PITFALLS
Team can regard creating the Flow Chart as their sole goal -- losing sight of purpose	The purposes of drawing the column flow chart are under "why use it" and "potentials" on pages 41 and 44. Discuss these before starting. *Be clear about team goals. Keep those goals in view, always.*
Can be involved	As a general rule, keep the number of activities in a column to four or less, then output to another column. *This assures a high level flow.* You may reenter the first column to draw more activities, but that set should be four or less, etc.
Difficult to decide, for some situations, where process begins and ends	Point out to the team that deciding boundaries is one of the key reasons for teams to use this tool. Make a decision for now.
Activity boxes can have multiple inputs; and/or multiple outputs	Multiple inputs and outputs for activity boxes are acceptable. For macro-flow charts, such as a column flow chart, avoid decision diamonds (these are discussed with the intermediate-level flow chart).
Process can have multiple inputs; real time and basic	Multiple inputs are acceptable. The process may be sufficiently complex that multiple inputs are present. Capture them. Be clear what they are and if they are *real-time* (raw material, data, or information that is changed by the process), or *basic* (inputs that are needed but not changed by the process, such as equipment, skills, resources, etc.). More on these in the "Construction" section.
Team members can have varied opinions on the actual work flow	If consensus is not yet possible, *capture the different views* of the flow. Show them on separate charts, or on one chart *using different colors.* Discuss the flows with others outside your team. Collect data. Come back to resolve the differences later.

from these Learn Pitfalls

<u>NOTES</u>

My Ideas and Items to practice at the next team meeting

THE CUSTOMER PAYMENT PROCESS

CASHIER	MANAGER	CUSTOMER (SHOPPER)

Shopper
Items → REVIEW PRICE ON ITEMS
Review
Sheets
Labels
Staff → ENTER PRICE
Stockers → BAG AND RECEIVE PAYMENT

DETERMINE PRICE

APPROVE CHECK

PAYMENT

Items bagged and paid

Shopper

———————— Real-time Input
·-·-·-·-·-·- Basic Input

NOTES

HOW TO CONSTRUCT A COLUMN FLOW CHART

1. Refer to the <u>Customer-Process-Supplier Model</u> below:
   a. Place your Process in the center. Identify the Customer(s) and Supplier(s). Then identify Inputs and Outputs.

   b. If there are multiple outputs from the process, select one.

   CPS MODEL

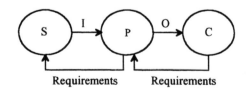

   S —I→ P —O→ C

   Requirements   Requirements

My Ideas and Items to practice at the next team meeting

► Different outputs mean different strings of subprocesses within the area being considered.

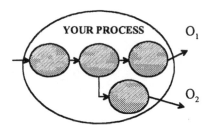

► The objective is to have the team work on one output, and therefore one clearly defined string of subprocesses.

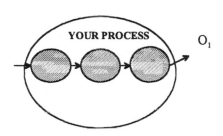

c. Identify the <u>real-time</u> inputs; those that are changed by the process, such as data, raw material, or information.

d. Identify the <u>basic</u> inputs; those that are required for the process to operate but are not changed by it, such as skills, resources, equipment, forms, invoice labels, records, etc. This can be a long list. Keep it to a minimum at this time.

e. Write the purpose of the process. Title the process.

> ☑ *Tip: The above steps a-e clarify and establish the boundaries of the process for the team. Forming this common understanding is very important for the team's effective communication.*

My Ideas and Items to practice at the next team meeting

2. Draw a box. Show the suppliers, inputs, customers, and the selected output.

    ☑ *Tip: The object in drawing the column flow chart is to draw the <u>actual</u> activities and flow.*

3. Identify the organizations, people, groups, or functional areas that are involved in converting the inputs into the output.

    ☑ *Tip: Cards that can be moved and changed are recommended here. The team can identify who is involved and place them in sequential order left to right by moving the cards.*

4. Draw the vertical columns, one for each organization.

NOTES

....

....

....

....

....

....

....

CASHIER	MANAGER	CUSTOMER (SHOPPER)

———————— Real-time Input

-·-·-·-·-·- Basic Input

5. Beginning with the input, identify the first activity.

    ► Each activity is a basic, high-level function. No decisions are shown. No detail.

    ☑ *Tip: Use cards for each activity. They can be moved.*

My Ideas and Items to practice at the next team meeting

....

....

☑   *Tip: If your team is uncertain whether the activity is too detailed, simply capture it and move on for now.*

6. Continue identifying activities, usually in the sequential order that they occur.

7. Connect the activity boxes.

    ▶   One activity may have multiple outputs or inputs. Single input or output arrows are not required.

    ☑   *Tip: Flow in the process may depend on what happens in a particular activity box, i.e., if 'A' happens there is one output, if 'B' then there is another. Simply show both. Decision boxes will be shown in the intermediate-level flow chart.*

    ☑   *Tip: Use different colored lines and arrows to show different flows that may happen. One input, for example, may generate one flow path, and another input generates another path.*

    ☑   *Tip: If generating this flow results in a different output than was originally identified by the teams, simply decide which you want, and be consistent in the CPS model. You may have to go back to change the CPS model and other plans.*

8. Take the <u>column flow chart</u> to stakeholders - people who work inside the process, or even customers and suppliers. Ask their views.

    ▶   Remember that any flow chart is intended to represent what happens. It is a picture of the facts; it is data. Ask stakeholders if they have different data, or different views. Follow up their differing views with data gathering.

    ☑   *Tip: Stakeholders may be affected by changes you make to the process. Obtaining their buy-in and support early is important.*

9. The <u>column flow chart</u> is a living document. It will serve as a guide throughout the team's efforts. In particular, a column flow chart can reveal.

My Ideas and Items to practice at the next team meeting

....

NOTES

....

....

....

....

....

....

a. Subprocesses, and the internal flows and hand-offs among those subprocesses.

b. The people in charge of each column of subprocesses are the **subprocess owners**. Consider having these people on your team.

c. Difficulties in the flow, as discussed further in Chapter 4.

> ► Look for duplication, unnecessary steps, and bottlenecks. Begin a list of possible opportunities or issues.

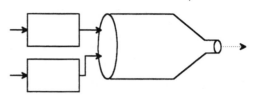

NOTES

> ► Identify areas that may need more flow detailing via an intermediate flow chart. This can be done now or at an appropriate later time.

d. Data collection points.

> ☑ *Tip: Remember that the flow arrows are just as important as the activity boxes. Errors or delays may happen on flow arrows and may need measuring.*

e. Streamlined flow as the process is improved.

My Ideas and Items to practice at the next team meeting

Column Flow Chart

for

Medication Order Process

in a Hospital Setting

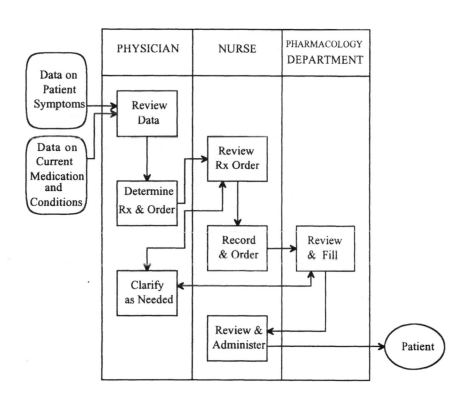

....

....

....

....

....

....

....

My Ideas and Items to practice at the next team meeting

....

. ...

NOTES

·····································

·····································

·····································

·····································

·····································

Column Flow Chart
for
Box Manufacturing

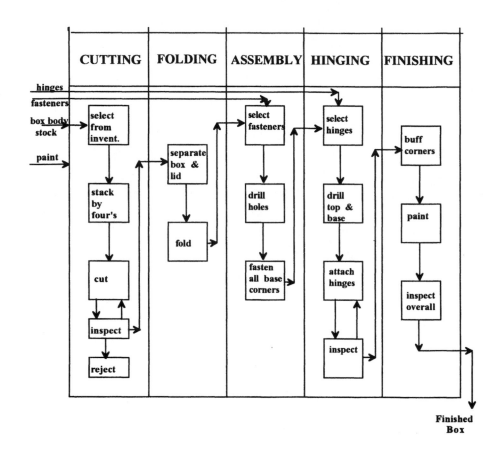

My Ideas and Items to practice at the next team meeting

······ ····· ··· ····· · ····· ··· ··· ···· ····· ···· ···· ·········· ·········· ····· ····· ······ ········· ····· ·········· ······· ······· ····· ·········

··· ···· ·· · ·· ·············· ····· ······· ······· ········ ···· ··· ···· ···· ················ ·········· ······· ···· ··········

When you have to make a choice and don't make it,
that in itself is a choice.
--William James

I am not a creator !

I merely separate out some local pattern from a confusing whole.

Buckminster Fuller

Award winning designer
and architect. Designer of
Geodesic Domes.
1895 - 1983

3

SITUATION:

Team Members Say -

"We need to streamline this process, and we need a more detailed flow than the column chart now."

"To take measurements, we need to draw the detailed flow and pick measurement points."

"Let's remember that this process has some time-eaters in it somewhere. We need to reduce these delays. Let's take a closer look at the flow."

SOLUTION:

Basic (Intermediate-Level) Flow Chart

Education is a progressive discovery of our ignorance.
--Will Durant

Basic Flow Chart

What Is It:

A flow of activities and decisions. The flow begins with some input - like data, or material - and ends with an output - a finished product or service to the customer.

Why Use It:

- To make *visible* the inside workings of a process
- To *uncover* inefficient flows, such as bottlenecks and repetitive loops
- To identify possible *measurements points*, and the type of data available at those points
- To capture the types of *decisions* being made in the business process and the information needed to make those decisions
- To prepare for *interviews* and gathering requirements from customers
- To prepare for *benchmarking* site visits at other organizations

When:

- Generally, after the boundaries, organizations, and basic elements of the process have been made visible via a column flow chart
- Useful before interviewing customers
- In preparation for planning data collection inside the process

FLOW CHARTS ARE KEY TOOLS

THEY MAKE OUR PROCESS VISIBLE

<u>TYPES OF FLOW CHARTS</u>

NOTES

• **MACRO FLOW CHART**

Shows the flow of a process at high level.   Generally no decision boxes; only activities.

• **COLUMN FLOW CHART**

A high level or macro flow chart, in which the activities are placed in columns that represent the organization (departments, groups, people) involved.

• **BASIC (INTERMEDIATE-LEVEL) FLOW CHART**

Show the details taking place within the high level activities of a macro flow chart. Decision boxes are present. Fairly detailed steps shown.

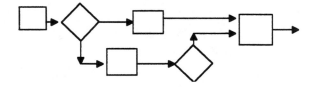

• **MICRO FLOW CHART**

Shows every movement involved in an activity or decision. Used especially in time and motion studies and in very detailed analysis.

My Ideas and Items to practice at the next team meeting

QUICK VIEW

BASIC FLOW CHART

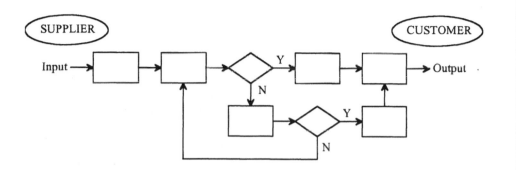

1. Determine output and customer.

2. Determine input and supplier.

3. Determine first activity or first decision.

4. Continue the flow until the specified output results.

5. Entire flows can be done with only activity boxes and decision diamonds.

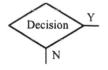

My Ideas and Items to practice at the next team meeting

Achieve these Potentials

NOTES

....

....

....

....

....

....

....

POTENTIALS	ACHIEVING POTENTIALS
Communication between Work Units improves	As team members begin to draw the flow chart, often the work that you or, other members, do is not clear. Invite fellow team members to visit your work area. Bring the flow chart. Discuss hand-offs and internal requirements. *Team communication will grow stronger!*
Decisions made in the process become clear	After seeing the decisions made in the process via "decision diamonds", identify the information needed for accurate and complete decisions to be made and plan to collect data on what information is *actually* available.
A living document	As with the column flow chart, this flow chart can be used to record improvements in activities, decisions, and flow. Show it to stakeholders, invite ideas and analysis.
Facilitates analysis for improvement (See chapter on "Tools for Analyzing Flow Charts")	Estimate actual times needed for activities and decisions, then compare those to actual times. This can reveal opportunities for reducing the overall cycle time or response time of the process. Likewise, look for bottlenecks, points of high error rates, unnecessary steps, holding patterns and places where items are inadvertently forgotten or lost. Place colored dots on the chart for data collection points that will be used to verify error rates, holding patterns, etc. *Planning for data collection comes alive!*
Partnerships begin with Supplier	Work with your supplier. Share the flow chart. Explain what you do with their input and what your customer wants. Ask you supplier for ideas, can they help you satisfy your customer? *Partnerships are powerful!*
Partnership begins with Customers	Discuss, with your customer, the objectives you have in improving the process. They may be able to help. They may not need or want everything the process sends to them. Also, you and your customer may find new ways, through coordination of your processes, to better satisfy the customer of your customer.

My Ideas and Items to practice at the next team meeting

....

....

PITFALLS	AVOIDING PITFALLS
Excessive time spent making the chart	"Use the Tool, do not let the Tool use you." Understand your *goal* as a team in using the flow chart, remind yourselves of it, at each step. If differences in opinion of process flow arise, document both or get information from others outside the team. If both paths are documented, simply come back to the issue later. Move on for now if at all possible.
Excessive level of detail in the chart	Decide as a team why you need this flow chart. Go back to your original goals as a team, if necessary. Perhaps your goal is to reduce time, or reduce errors, or increase through put, or reduce volume from suppliers, or reduce complexity. Make a list. The objective of drawing and using the flow chart will guide the team in the level of detail needed. For example, the team wonders if they should show every hand-off and repeated hand-off of a document between two people in a work unit. If time reduction is an objective, yes. If throughput is an objective, yes, again. If reduction of unnecessary inputs from suppliers is the objective, or improving how the process provides accurate status information to customers, then perhaps that detail is unnecessary at this time. If in doubt, start at the easiest level to draw - whichever is more natural to represent.

from Learn *these* *Pitfalls*

NOTES

....

....

....

....

....

....

My Ideas and Items to practice at the next team meeting

....

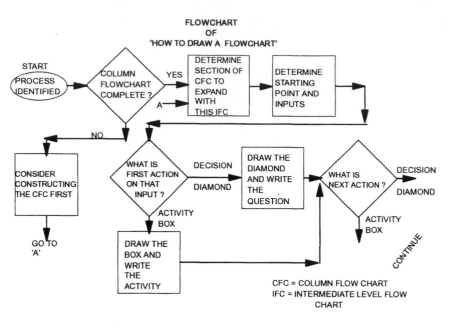

FLOWCHART
OF
'HOW TO DRAW A FLOWCHART'

CFC = COLUMN FLOW CHART
IFC = INTERMEDIATE LEVEL FLOW CHART

NOTES

HOW TO CONSTRUCT AN INTERMEDIATE-LEVEL FLOW CHART

1. With two symbols used in flow charting, you can draw virtually anything: These two symbols are:

   a. <u>Activity Box</u> - shows an <u>action taken</u>. Each activity box normally has one output, but may have multiple inputs. If a box has multiple outputs of different types, you need to consider dividing the activity box into more detail. Multiple and different outputs imply different intermediate activities. Our objective here is to identify those different activities.

   b. <u>Decision Diamond</u> - asks a question and shows different outputs as a result of the answer, or decision. Usually "yes" or "no".

My Ideas and Items to practice at the next team meeting

2. Another useful symbol is the <u>Start/Stop Ellipse</u> - used to show when a process begins or ends. The <u>start</u> usually contains a brief description of what comes into (inputs) the process, and the <u>stop</u> contains the output.

 or, for more room to write words, use this symbol

3. Begin at the top center of the page, or at the left side, as you choose, and draw the <u>start</u> symbol. Place in it the event that starts the process and the <u>real-time</u> input (data, materials, items, etc.) that flow into the process and are changed by it. <u>Basic</u> inputs can also be shown. (See the description of the column flow chart for more on real-time and basic inputs.)   EXAMPLE :

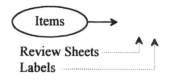

☑ *Tip: Remember that you are, throughout this flow chart, drawing the actual flow of activities and decisions you can observe. The input begins the flow of those observable, real events.*

4. Determine the first action or decision that is taken and draw a box or diamond for it. Continue by asking:

What is the output of this?
Who receives it?
What happens next?

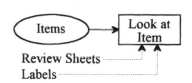

5. Simply continue stepping through your process, drawing activity boxes and decision diamonds as needed, and the flow among them.

6. When complete, place a title on the flow chart that describes the process.

My Ideas and Items to practice at the next team meeting

☑   *Tip: If this is an expansion of the entire <u>column flow chart</u>, it would be titled the same.*

☑   *Tip: If it is an expansion of only part of the whole process, then choose a title that describes the subprocess or set of subprocesses involved.*

7. Analyze the flow chart.

    a. Look for repetition, bottlenecks, activities with high errors, unnecessary steps, and pits or deep holes where items are lost.

    b. Ask stakeholders their view (see column flow chart for suggestions in this area).

    c. Draw a more efficient version of how the process could flow and compare the two. How long, for example, does the actual take, and how long would the new design take? Can time be saved with the new design? Are their tradeoffs, such as less time but likelihood of more errors?

    d. See the chapter here on 'Analyzing Flow Charts,' Chapter 4.

8. General comments.

    a. Flow charts are an art, not a perfect science. Use your imagination and judgment. If the flow is an accurate depiction of the facts, that is what matters, not the style.

    b. You can elaborate on your intermediate-level flow chart by placing the various activity boxes and decision into the organization columns of the column flow chart. This is sometimes useful for seeing hand-offs between organizations.

    c. Use this flow chart to identify measurement points, as with a column flow chart.

NOTES

My Ideas and Items to practice at the next team meeting

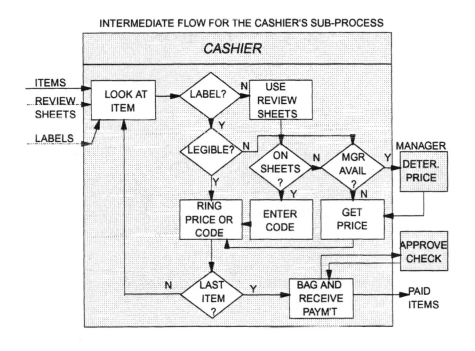

INTERMEDIATE FLOW FOR THE CASHIER'S SUB-PROCESS

NOTES

....

....

....

....

....

....

....

My Ideas and Items to practice at the next team meeting

....

Intermediate Flow Chart

for

Medication Order Process

in a Hospital Setting

NOTES

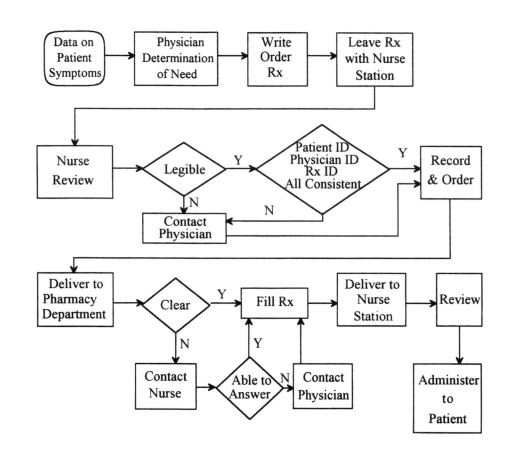

My Ideas and Items to practice at the next team meeting

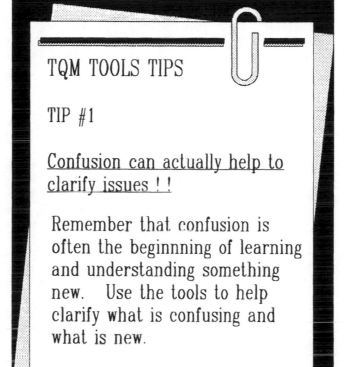

TQM TOOLS TIPS

TIP #1

<u>Confusion can actually help to clarify issues ! !</u>

Remember that confusion is often the beginnning of learning and understanding something new.   Use the tools to help clarify what is confusing and what is new.

He who stops being better, stops being good.

Oliver Cromwell
British Statesman
1599 -1658

4

SITUATION:

Team Members Say -

"Great flow chart. Now what?"

"Well, I can tell from this flow chart that the process has problems - but I am not sure what those problems are or how they affect the customer."

"Also, we need to figure out how to streamline the flow of this process."

SOLUTION:

Tools for Analyzing Flow Charts

THIS CHAPTER PROVIDES TOOLS AND IDEAS FOR ANALYZING FLOW CHARTS. THERE ARE TWO PARTS TO THIS CHAPTER:

TABLES FOR ANALYZING FLOW CHART DATA

1. Draw column flow chart.

2. Identify subprocesses.

3. Construct an *Internal/External Customer Requirements Table*, shown on page 74 here.

4. Determine (a) bottlenecks, (b) repetitive loops, (c) points of likely high errors, (d) unnecessary steps, and (e) steps that can be changed for smoother flow (such as changing who does a step, or when).

5. Draw Intermediate-Level Flow chart (IFC).

6. Construct *Analysis Table* of the items flowing through the IFC, as shown on page 75 here.

   Note: The Analysis Table will show measurements and actual data related to the type of improvement you arc trying to make. It will show, for example, time to accomplish activities (if time is the issue), or errors that result from activities (if errors are the issue).

7. Collect data to support the Analysis Table.

8. Display and Analyze the Data.

9. List conclusions and plan next step.

My Ideas and Items to practice at the next team meeting

The following example demonstrates the analysis of a set of flow charts from a medication ordering process.

MACRO FLOW CHART

FOR

MEDICATION ORDER PROCESS

IN A HOSPITAL SETTING

NOTES

| PHYSICIAN WRITES Rx | → | NURSE REVIEWS Rx ORDER | → | PHARMACO-LOGY DEPT FILLS Rx | → | PATIENT RECEIVES Rx |

Customer (Patient) Requirement: Accurate medication, delivered on time.

The Problem Area: Late delivery of medication to patients.

Approach: Begin analysis and data collection planning via a Column Flow Chart and Intermediate-Level Flow Chart.

My Ideas and Items to practice at the next team meeting

COLUMN FLOW CHART

FOR MEDICATION ORDER PROCESS

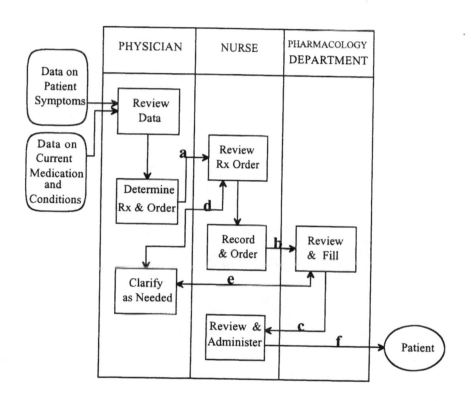

My Ideas and Items to practice at the next team meeting

Table of Internal/External Customer Requirements

Subprocess Output	Customer	Customer Requirements	Customer Target	Perceived Actuals	Perceived Gap
a - Physician Order	Nurse	Clarity	100%	Most are Clear	Small
b - Nurse Order	Pharmacist	Clarity Timely	100% 45 min.	Most are Clear Most are Timely	Small Small
c - Pharmacist Fill	Nurse	Timely Accurate Complete	2 hours 100% 100%	Late OK OK	Medium None None
d - Physician Clarification	Nurse	Time	5 min.	- Long periods to reach MD - Several each day	Large
e - Physician Clarification	Pharmacist	Time	5 min.	- Long periods to reach MD - Many each day	Large
f - Administer	Patient	Accurate Complete Timely		OK OK Some Delays	None None Medium

Analysis from the Customer Table:

1. Perception is that the 'Clarification' subprocess outputs (d) & (e) may be time-eaters.

   This steers the team to mark these subprocess outputs as a place to collect data.

2. The 'Administer' subprocess output activity (f) may also be responsible for delays. The team can consider data collection there, either now or later.

   Note, however, that the 'medium' delays patients perceive at (f) are probably caused by, or certainly related to, the 'large' delays that occur at (d,) or (e).

Next Step:

   Construct an Intermediate-Level Flow Chart to make visible the difficulties that can occur with (d) and (e).

My Ideas and Items to practice at the next team meeting

Time Analysis Table

for the

Intermediate-Level Flow Chart

Medication Order Process

ACTIVITY	NO. OF ITEMS	IDEAL TIME TO HANDLE	ACTUAL TIME REQUIRED	DIFFERENCE
d	2 to 20/day	5 minutes each, maximum	5-120 minutes each	0-115 minutes
e	5 to 10/day	5 minutes each, maximum	10-65 minutes each	5-60 minutes

Note: The above data was collected over a ten day period. Each day, the number of items were counted and the time required to handle each item was recorded.

Results of this Analysis of Flow Charts:

The Internal/External Customer Requirements Table and the Analysis Table have provided information that enables us to write this <u>Problem Statement</u>:

The Medication Order Process has a bottleneck at the 'clarify as needed' activity that involves up to 30 items each day requiring up to two hours each for resolution. Reduction of the number of items and of the response time will have a noticeable positive impact for up to 30 patients each day.

Typical Next Step:

Collect data on each type of occurrence when a physician is contacted for clarification. A check sheet would be a simple way to record the data. Here is one way to structure such a check sheet:

<u>*NOTES*</u>

My Ideas and Items to practice at the next team meeting

Type of question for clarification with MD:	Time Required to Resolve (Minutes)							
	5-10	10-20	20-40	40-60	60-80	80-100	100-120	120-140
Illegible	lll	lllll	l	llll	lll		l	l
Wrong Patient	ll	l						
Allergy Indic.	l			l				
Wrong Date	ll		l		l	l		
Missing Info.		lllll	ll	lllll	llll		llll	lll
Other	ll	lll	ll	lll	lll		ll	l

Other types of data can be collected for the questions that need clarification by physicians:

❑   Time of day - morning, afternoon, evening, night, late night.

   o   Do most of the questions on prescriptions happen at a certain period of the day?

   o   Is the response time much longer for some period, like late night?

❑   Day of week

   o   Is there a pattern of more occurrences by day of week?

❑   Physicians

   o   Perhaps contacting a few physicians cause 80% of the delay - the Pareto Principle.

This data can be displayed with a variety of charts:

- Pareto (types of questions, the physicians, etc.)
- Histogram (time to resolve)
- Scatter Diagram (time of day vs. time to resolve)
- Pie Chart (proportion of types of questions, etc.)
- Bar Chart (number of questions by day of week or by time of day, etc.)
- Run Chart (one curve for each type of question showing the trend by time of day, or by day of week, or even by physician)

My Ideas and Items to practice at the next team meeting

OPTIMIZING PROCESSES

BY

ANALYZING FLOW CHART

Optimization falls into two categories: **Avoiding Accommodation Functions**, and **Taking Constructive Actions** to streamline the flow.

Avoiding Accommodation Functions
Accommodation functions compensate for activities not performed well in the process. If an activity in a process is not performing efficiently, or in a way that does not generate the desired output, then an *accommodation function* may occur later because it is needed.

To avoid accommodation functions occurring in your process, you first need to recognize them. Here is a list of accommodation functions:

Inspection
Is inspection present to compensate for poor upstream performance? Do not design for long term inspection points simply to compensate. If an inspection point is finding a 2% error level, work upstream to reduce that to 1%, and then 0.1%.

Storing
Has the process been designed to hold or store an item until the next activity is ready? Design the activity that follows the storage to be faster. Perhaps duplicate it. If it is a slow and detailed activity, you may have an unavoidable bottleneck. It is often wise to place an inspection point in front of such an activity to assure that only acceptable items flow into it. It is too costly and valuable a step to have poor product entering it.

Transferring
Inside your process, is there transferring of information from one sheet to another, or the moving of a product from one container to another? This may be unnecessary.

Duplicating
Is your process making multiple copies of information sheets, or placing data sets into two different formats for two different user groups within the overall process? This may be unnecessary.

Correcting
How much accommodation is done correcting errors? How much time and money is spent? The rework that comes from finding errors during inspection is costly. It is even more costly if the customer experiences the error. Work to reduce this activity.

My Ideas and Items to practice at the next team meeting

NOTES

Locating

How much time is spent locating items? If data or materials are not easy to find, process activities will be diverted from efficient efforts to fairly long time periods locating needed items. Design the process such that items are easy to track and locate.

Transporting

How much time is spent transporting items throughout the process? The arrows between the activities represents this transportation. It may take considerable time to transport an item. Design your processes to provide the fastest transport while not overlooking other requirements such as safety, accuracy, and cost.

Take Constructive Actions

Here are a set of constructive actions to consider when optimizing your process:

❑ Eliminate activities. Can an activity, or part of it, be removed. Ask if each activity is:

> *Separate, Unique, and Necessary (SUNny).* In other words, each activity is not repeating what is done elsewhere in the process, is not overlapping, and is needed to generate the output.

❑ Whenever possible, and cost effective, design activities to be done in parallel. That is, consider having separate activities done *simultaneously* if possible, rather than one after another.

❑ Consider having activities work on *batches* of items rather than on individual items. Using batches requires waiting for, say, five items to arrive at the front-end of an activity before the activity begins. If the activity is simple, fast, and efficient, and if the operators of the activity can be doing other processing for something else while the batch is forming, this is often an efficient strategy.

My Ideas and Items to practice at the next team meeting

I find the great thing in this world is not so much
where we stand, as in what direction we are moving:
To reach the port of heaven, we must sail sometimes
with the wind and sometimes against it, but we must
sail, and not drift, nor lie at anchor.
--Oliver Wendell Holmes

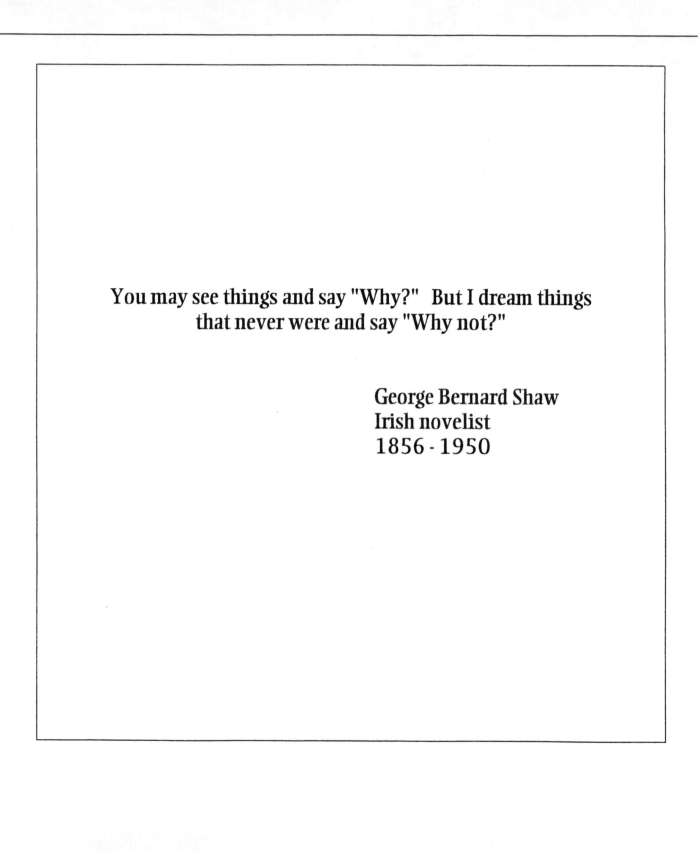

You may see things and say "Why?" But I dream things
that never were and say "Why not?"

George Bernard Shaw
Irish novelist
1856 - 1950

5

SITUATION:

Team Members Say -

"*Maybe - just maybe - we need to find out clearly what our customers want.*"

"*What are our customers measuring on the products or service we are giving them?*"

"*What do our customers want us to measure?*"

"*Are our customers satisfied? Can we measure that?*"

SOLUTION:

Customer Requirements Matrix

The best way out is always through.
--Robert Frost

Customer Requirements Matrix

What Is It:

A matrix, or table, for capturing customer needs in specific terms. It can be used with internal or external customers.

Why Use It:

- To provide a structured but flexible means to capture the important elements of customer needs in *measurable* ways
- To serve as a guide when *planning* customer interviews or surveys
- To serve as a guide *during* the interview process
- To *summarize* your customer's requirements and guide your process improvement efforts

When:

- Especially useful during the early discussions with customers
- During team discussions about internal work flow requirements
- During interviews, as a way to document needs
- Understanding customer needs is an ongoing process

Let us not be content to wait and see what will happen,
but give us the determination to make the right things
happen.
--Peter Marshall

QUICK VIEW

CUSTOMER REQUIREMENTS MATRIX

Output	Quality Character-istics	Description	What to Measure	Target	Importance to Customer	Customer View of Gap	Rank

Quality Characteristics include:

- Accuracy
- Clarity
- Durability
- Completeness
- Application
- Reliability
- Timeliness
- Ease of Use
- Purity

1. Identify the primary output associated with the process.

2. Identify quality characteristics as broad categories.

3. The customer describes a particular item, or more than one, for each quality characteristic.

4. Determine what the customer wants you to measure for each described item, such as "days".

5. The customer describes the target for the measurement, such as "less than five days".

6. On a scale of 1 to 5, capture the importance of each item to the customer: 1= low, 5 = high.

7. On a scale of 1 to 5, capture the customer perceived gap: 1 = small, 5 = large.

8. The rank is the product of the importance and the perceived gap.

My Ideas and Items to practice at the next team meeting

NOTES

POTENTIALS	ACHIEVING POTENTIALS
Form ongoing dialog with Customers	Use the flow chart, data display tools, etc., to show customers your intentions. Ask for their views, their ideas. Use the Customer Requirements Matrix (CRM) to *plan* the interview before actually meeting with the customer. Fill it out as best you can as a team before the interview as practice. Use the CRM during the interview. Show it to the customer. Arrange to return to finish areas that cannot be completed the first time.
Begin a Progressive Interaction with Customers	Four basic phases of progressive interaction can be developed. As a team, be aware of these phases and work to transition from one to another. ►**The Interview** Here, we meet with the customer to gather information and to enter it in the CRM. We learn <u>what</u> to measure from the customer's viewpoint. Our challenge, as a team, will be <u>how</u> to effectively measure what the customer wants, i.e., the method for collecting the data. ►**Negotiations** After hearing the customer, and returning to collect data on the process, we often better understand the capabilities of the process at present. We may need to negotiate time frames with the customer on when process changes will be made. ►**Benchmarking** Often it is useful to understand what your customer can find in the marketplace. This phase involves discussions not only with your customer about what they have experienced but also with other organizations and businesses about their processes. ►**Partnering** As the ultimate interaction with your customer, this phase is exemplified by asking your customer <u>why</u> they want a product or service from you. Put another way, you can ask your customer to explain the products and services <u>their</u> customer wants. Then explore ways that your process and your customer's process can work together as one.

Achieve *these* **Potentials**

NOTES

....

....

....

....

....

....

My Ideas and Items to practice at the next team meeting

....

....

PITFALLS	AVOIDING PITFALLS
Time and Cost	Interviewing customers takes time, especially if they are external customers and travel time is required. Customer information is vital, but so is your time and theirs. Here are some guidelines to help balance the time and cost with the benefit:

from these Learn - Pitfalls

► **Planning**
Before interviewing the customer:

- Understand, clearly, the purpose of the interview. Discuss it as a team. Write it.
- Write your questions. Coordinate them with the CRM.
- Role-play the interview with other team members.
- Establish a length of time for the interview.
- Decide which team members will visit the customer. Two are recommended because they can alternate asking questions and writing responses. One can ask while the other writes, then reverse.

► **Scheduling**
Set a time with your customer and adhere to it. Ask for more time later, if necessary.

► **Summarizing**
Conclude the interview with a summary of the CRM. Check for clarity and accuracy with the customer. Also conclude with an agreement on when you will respond back to the customer on any open items or questions that arose during the sessions.

► **Reviewing**
After returning to the team workplace, review the interview process to uncover ways to improve it next time.

NOTES

Customers may expect improvements after being asked for their needs	Review the four phases of progressive interaction with customers, shown above under "Achieving Potentials." Be certain, during the *interview* phase, that the customer understands that you are basically only gathering information. Negotiation, or discussion on what your process can deliver, will come later. Discuss your plans with the customer.

My Ideas and Items to practice at the next team meeting

CUSTOMER REQUIREMENTS MATRIX

FOR

CLAIMS PAYMENT PROCESS

Output	Quality Characteristic	Description	What to Measure	Target	Importance to Customer	Customer View of Gap	Rank
Payment on a Claim	Accuracy	Correct Amount	Dollars	Zero Deviation from Covered Charges	5	1*	5
	Timeliness	Time from Sending the Claim until Payment	Days	10 or Less	4	5	20
	Understand-able	Explanation of not Covered Charges is Clear and Believable	Number of Unclear Points	Zero	5	3	15

*Note: A "1" in this example means the customer sees essentially no gap. A high gap is 5, meaning there is a large difference between what they want and what they are receiving.

My Ideas and Items to practice at the next team meeting

....

....

Using

the

Customer Requirements Matrix

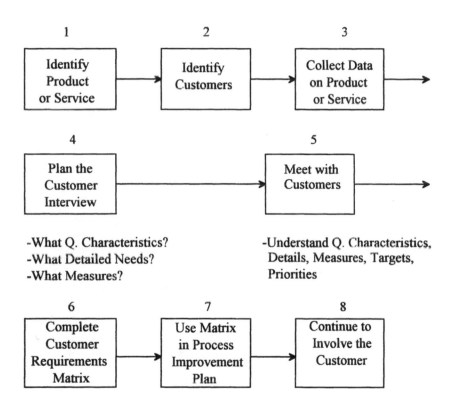

My Ideas and Items to practice at the next team meeting

....

In God we trust. All others must use data.

W. Edwards Deming
TQM expert and advocate
1900 - 1993

6

SITUATION:

Team Members Say -

“What should we use -

- **a bar chart**
- **a line chart**
- **a pie chart**
- **a radar chart**
- **or something else?”**

SOLUTION:

Guidelines on selection of Data Display Charts

GENERAL INFORMATION ON DATA DISPLAY CHARTS AND GRAPHS

Charts and graphs for displaying data are not as complicated as most people think. Once we realize that there are several common features across all data display charts and graphs, we can see how to construct and use them effectively and easily.

There are three basic types of data charts used in process improvement team efforts: Pie, X-Y axis, and Radar. The " X-Y axis " category is composed of several different charts, as shown on this <u>tree diagram</u> .

NOTES

....

....

....

....

....

....

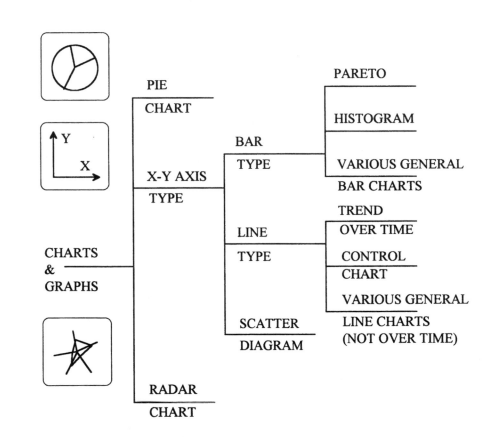

My Ideas and Items to practice at the next team meeting

....

....

Let's see what we can learn from just this tree diagram:

1. Pie charts are simple. There are no special or different versions; there are only differences in the level of detail that can be shown. Three dimensional pie charts are a different style; not different information. Pie charts have the advantage of being simple. Also, they show a snap-shot in time, a static state, rather than patterns over time.

2. X-Y charts are of only three basic types: Bar, line, and scatter. (Three-dimensional surface charts are really extensions of line charts.) Our decision on what type of X-Y chart to use is simplified by the fact that there are only three basic types!

3. Radar charts show measurements outward from the center. Larger values are at the edge and each ray, or line, from the center represents one variable or item being measured. As the tree diagram shows, there is only one type of radar chart. The name, by the way, comes from the pattern that is created - it looks like a radar screen pattern.

Since the X-Y type of chart offers the most choices, let's look for the common features among all X-Y charts. There are four basic points concerning the items on the vertical (Y) and horizontal (X) axis.

Vertical Axis

1. The vertical axis typically shows one of a few basic categories:

VERTICAL AXIS TYPICAL CATEGORIES

CATEGORY	EXAMPLES
Frequency of an event	Number of errors; number of calls; number of people; number of complaints
Length	Inches, feet, miles, etc.
Volume	Gallons, cubic feet, etc.
Percent	Proportion of the whole
Cost	Dollar cost of capital, repair, installation, rework, lost future sales , etc.
Savings	Dollar savings of correcting a problem, avoiding an expense, etc.

2. The vertical axis generally shows the <u>dependent</u> variable. This is the frequency, volume, cost, etc., that <u>results</u> from events or other given (independent) items shown on the horizontal axis.

My Ideas and Items to practice at the next team meeting

NOTES

<u>Horizontal Axis</u>

1. The horizontal axis also typically shows one of a few basic categories:

HORIZONTAL AXIS TYPICAL CATEGORIES

CATEGORY	EXAMPLES
Measurable Value	Time, dollars, length, volume, weight. Typically used on a bar chart or trend chart or control chart.
Events or Category	Types of errors, type of request, name, location in a process, etc. Typically used on a Pareto chart or a bar chart.
Measurement Intervals	Intervals of any measurement, such as height, time to complete a task, level of cholesterol, etc. Typically used on a Histogram.

2. The horizontal axis is the <u>independent</u> variable. It is set or given. The question is, when the independent variable (the tenth hour, for example) happens, what is the resultant dependent variable (number of calls, for example).

HOW TO SELECT THE BEST CHART FOR YOUR DATA

There are several points to make about selecting a chart to display your data:

1. Often there is no single right choice. Any one of several charts could be used. Feel free to experiment and to express your own style.

2. Understand the goal you have in displaying the data.   Is it to make a point, and what is that point? Or is it to see patterns so that you can make a decision?

3. Before selecting a chart, make a sketch of what you think it will look like in final form. Sketch others as well. Select one based on the one that you think best displays the points you wish to make about the data, or any other goal you have.

The following tree diagram has been useful in helping teams select the most effective chart to construct:

My Ideas and Items to practice at the next team meeting

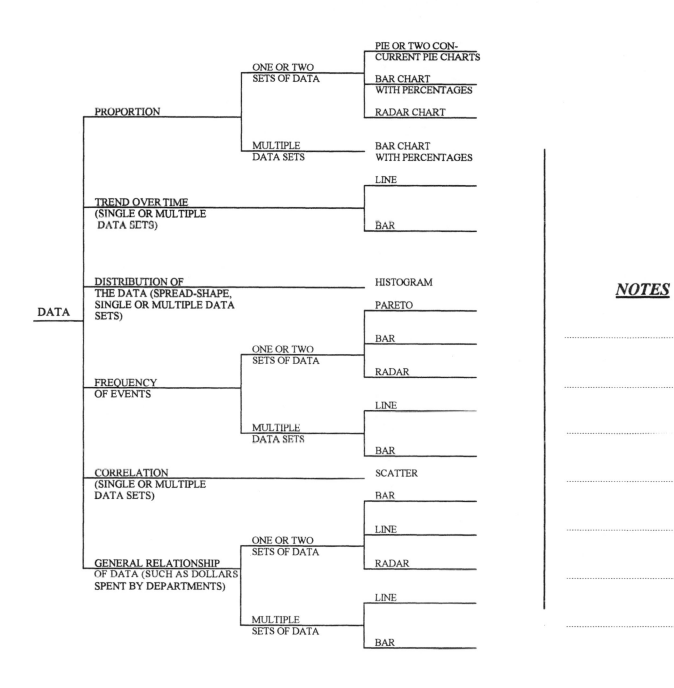

NOTES

My Ideas and Items to practice at the next team meeting

NOTES

Note: When two charts are listed at the end of the tree diagram, the top one is usually preferred, based on clarity, simplicity, and impact for the given subject of interest to the team. For example, a pie chart is generally preferred and recommended over a bar chart to show proportions.

First-time teams working to improve service-oriented processes tend to prefer a few specific types of charts. Further, these few charts have proven to be effective for those teams. Data from over 130 first-time service-oriented teams over a five-year period is displayed in this Pareto format:

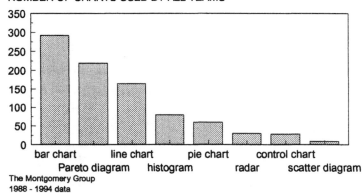

DATA-DISPLAY CHARTS
USED BY FIRST-TIME TEAMS
NUMBER OF CHARTS USED BY ALL TEAMS

The Montgomery Group
1988 - 1994 data

As teams progress, they become more comfortable with histograms, control charts, and scatter diagrams. A Pareto for experienced teams would show those bars to be higher.

In summary, to select a type of chart to display your data:

- Use the tree diagram on page 4-5 above to select the type of chart.

- If an X-Y chart is selected--that is, a bar chart, line graph, or scatter diagram--use the tables of typical categories for vertical and horizontal axes on pages 4-3 and 4-4 above to explore the labels and units on the X and Y axes.

And, remember: Experiment! Use your ideas and your opinions. There is no single right way to display data!

My Ideas and Items to practice at the next team meeting

TQM TOOLS TIPS

TIP # 2

Use the tools, do not let the tools
use you ! !

Keep your ideas flowing and try
not to become bogged down in
details that are not important
for achieving your goals.

To find a fault is easy; to do better may be difficult.

Plutarch
Greek biographer
46 -120 A.D.

7

SITUATION:

Team Members Say -

"We need to show others the whole data picture in a simple way."

"We have the percentage each item is of the whole, and we need a simple way to see that."

"Proportionally, we have made significant improvement. Let's show that to our customers and suppliers in an overall picture."

SOLUTION:

Pie Chart

We are face to face with our destiny and we must meet it with a high and resolute courage. For us is the life of action, of strenuous performance of duty; let us live in the harness, striving mightily; let us rather run the risk of wearing out than rusting out.
--Theodore Roosevelt

Pie Chart

What Is It:

A pictorial display of the proportional occurrence of events or conditions.

Why Use It:

- To display *relative* data in quick, easily assimilated format
- To show the *proportion* of events/items/problems/etc.
- To assist in *determining* what to address within a process or a problem area

When:

- Displaying status and static state of a process rather than over time
- Anytime a display of proportional occurrences is useful
- May be used in place of a Pareto Diagram, although to do so is not conventional
- Useful during presentations and early exploration of process status

Only the educated are free.
--Epictetus

<u>*QUICK VIEW*</u>

<u>**PIE CHART**</u>

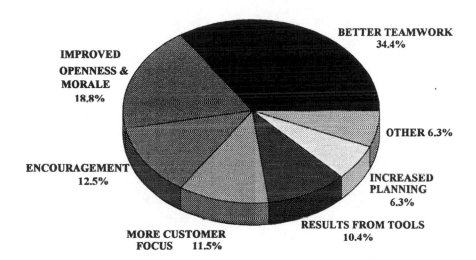

BETTER TEAMWORK
34.4%

IMPROVED
OPENNESS &
MORALE
18.8%

OTHER 6.3%

ENCOURAGEMENT
12.5%

INCREASED
PLANNING
6.3%

RESULTS FROM TOOLS
10.4%

MORE CUSTOMER
FOCUS   11.5%

<u>*NOTES*</u>

1. Collect data. Form categories for the data.

2. Order the category by size; the category with highest number of responses would be first.

3. Convert the numeric value of each category to a percent.

4. Divide the circle of the Pie according to the percent for each category.

5. Label the segments of the pie.

My Ideas and Items to practice at the next team meeting

POTENTIALS	ACHIEVING POTENTIALS
Multiple Pie Charts for different time periods	Suppose your team has measured the response of customers to the process output before making improvements, and after. The two responses can be shown side-by-side on pie charts. *SEE FIGURES A and B* As another example, suppose your company has four major processes, each of which generates a different service. The relative demand for services A, B, C, and D can be displayed for year 1 and year 2: *SEE FIGURES C*
Further breakdown of selected slices within the pie	A graphical advantage pie charts offer is to further divide a proportional piece into more detail.

NOTES

....

....

....

....

....

....

CUSTOMER RESPONSE
AFTER

Good   56.0%

External Customer
Excellent   15.0%

Internal Customer
Fair   3.0%

Satisfactory   26.0%

My Ideas and Items to practice at the next team meeting

....

....

these Achieve Potentials

CUSTOMER RESPONSE
BEFORE

Good 42.0%

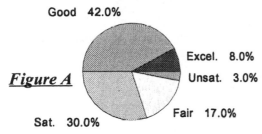

Excel. 8.0%

Unsat. 3.0%

Figure A

Fair 17.0%

Sat. 30.0%

CUSTOMER RESPONSE
AFTER

Good 56.0%

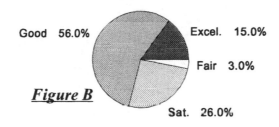

Excel. 15.0%

Fair 3.0%

Figure B

Sat. 26.0%

DEMAND FOR SERVICES

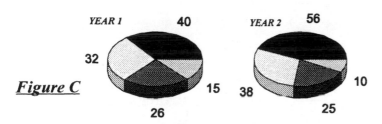

YEAR 1   40

32

Figure C

15

26

YEAR 2   56

38   10

25

■ A ▫ B ▨ C ▨ D

<u>REQUESTS SHOWN IN THOUSANDS</u>

My Ideas and Items to practice at the next team meeting

POTENTIALS	ACHIEVING POTENTIALS
Easily visualized and understood	Pie charts present an overall, total, and integrated picture. They do not allow easy quantitative visualization of the difference between two items - as a bar chart does - but they show the whole picture well.
Provide a diversion from Bar Charts, which are commonly used	Bar charts are frequently used in documents and presentations because they clearly show the difference between two values. Pie charts provide an alternative that can be sharp and to the point when the total picture needs to be seen. Compare these two charts that display the same data:

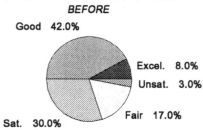

The *pie chart* shows proportions of each customer response compared to the whole. The *bar chart* makes visible relative levels rather than proportion.

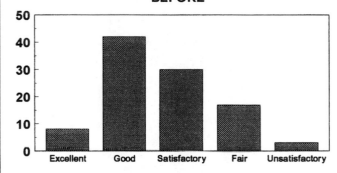

My Ideas and Items to practice at the next team meeting

....

....

NOTES

PITFALLS	AVOIDING PITFALLS
Difficult to see change between two Pie Charts, i.e. Year 1 to Year 2	Try a mockup of the pie chart first; and a bar chart sketch. Compare the two. Which makes your point better? Also, you might consider side-by-side pie charts with separated segments to help create a clear visualization of the change from one time period to another:

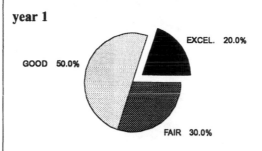

year 1

EXCEL. 20.0%
GOOD 50.0%
FAIR 30.0%

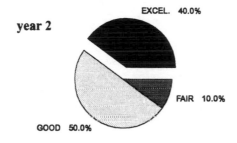

year 2

EXCEL. 40.0%
FAIR 10.0%
GOOD 50.0%

NOTES

Not as quantitative in displaying levels and differences between levels as a line graph or bar chart	When differences need to be clearly visible, or when relative levels are important to see, use a bar chart or line graph.

My Ideas and Items to practice at the next team meeting

PIE CHART OF TIME SPENT ON ACTIVITIES
IN THE CUSTOMER PAYMENT PROCESS

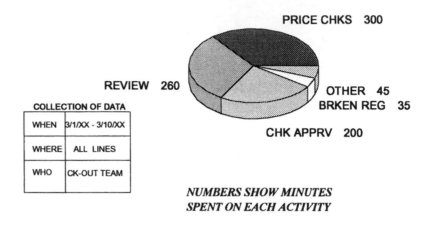

PRICE CHKS   300

REVIEW   260

OTHER   45
BRKEN REG   35

CHK APPRV   200

COLLECTION OF DATA	
WHEN	3/1/XX - 3/10/XX
WHERE	ALL LINES
WHO	CK-OUT TEAM

NUMBERS SHOW MINUTES
SPENT ON EACH ACTIVITY

NOTES

MANUAL SKETCH, OR COMPUTER GENERATION, OR BOTH?

Computer graphic programs today can usually construct a pie chart automatically. There are several reasons that the construction steps that follow can be useful *even if you have an automatic graph-generating program.*

► You may prefer your design over the predesigned, computer generated one. For example, you may want to place the segments in a certain order, or position, on the pie. You may want to use a computer drawing program to construct the pie chart you want.

► Sketch a chart as a draft of what can be expected. By doing such a draft, or mockup, you can understand the messages that will be communicated with the final product. Is it clear? Is this chart showing the message, or point, you want to make?

My Ideas and Items to practice at the next team meeting

► Probably the most important reason to manually arrange the data and construct a pie chart is the true understanding of the tool that results.

HOW TO CONSTRUCT A PIE CHART

1. Collect data on the subject. A check sheet is a simple, effective way to collect the data if you need to count the number of times each event happens. If you are measuring time, or dollars, for example, direct measures of each would be recorded. Make a table displaying the data, as in the example:

<u>Time Eaters in Customer Payment Process*</u>

Check Approved	200 minutes
Price Checks	300 minutes
Using Review Sheets	260 minutes
Broken Cash Register	35 minutes
Other	45 minutes

* Data gathered over a two-week period as customers wait in line, then proceed through the check-out and payment steps.

2. Now order the data, largest to smallest:

<u>Time Eaters in Customer Payment Process</u>

Price Checks	300 minutes
Using Review Sheets	260 minutes
Check Approval	200 minutes
Broken Cash Register	35 minutes
Other*	45 minutes

* 'Other' goes last even if it is larger than the category before it. None of the individual items in 'other', however, can be larger than the category before it (Broken Cash Register).

NOTES

My Ideas and Items to practice at the next team meeting

3. Next, decide the number of segments for your pie chart. You can change this later if you wish, but if you have many separate events, the pie chart may look cluttered. Generally, eight segments is a maximum for clarity.

> ☑ *Tip: If you have more measured items than segments that you want in your pie chart, combine the last (lowest volume) items into one category called "other."*

4. The objective now is to find the proportion that each item, or event, is of the total. Simply compute the percent each item is of the total.

<u>Time Eaters in Customer Payment Process</u>

Price Checks	36%
Using Review Sheets	31%
Check Approval	24%
Broken Cash Register	4%
Other	5%
	100%

NOTES

5. Now we use the percentages to divide the pie, or the circle, into segments.

Since a circle contains 360 degrees, we simply multiply the percentage for each item by 360. The result is the pie segment in degrees for each item.

<u>Time Eaters in Customer Payment Process</u>

Price Checks	36% x 360 = 130 degrees
Using Review Sheets	31% x 360 = 112 degrees
Check Approval	24% x 360 = 86 degrees
Broken Cash Register	4% x 360 = 14 degrees
Other	5% x 360 = 18 degrees
	360 degrees

6. Now construct the pie chart by dividing the pie into segments based on the degrees. Label each segment and show the percent for each.

7. Title the pie chart and show your data box that gives the date, who collected the data, and where.

My Ideas and Items to practice at the next team meeting

TIME SPENT IN CUSTOMER PAYMENT PROCESS

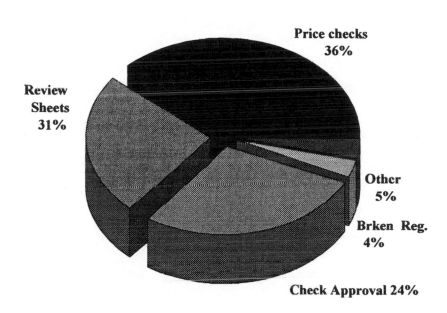

Price checks
36%

Review
Sheets
31%

Other
5%

Brken Reg.
4%

Check Approval 24%

Data Collection

3/1/xx to 3/10/xx
From All Service Lines
By the Check-out Team

My Ideas and Items to practice at the next team meeting

....

A person who makes no mistakes does not usually make anything.

Edward Phelps
Jounalist and author
1863 - 1915

8

SITUATION:

Team Members Say -

"Let's look closer at this data."

"Alright. Let's use a display that allows us to see small differences."

"Perhaps we need a simple graph that, at the same time, is quantitative - that is, shows and clearly compares data values."

SOLUTION:

Bar Chart

An education isn't how much you have committed to memory, or even how much you know. It's being able to differentiate between what you do know and what you don't.
--Anatole France

Bar Chart

What Is It:

Bar charts - showing either vertical or horizontal bars - are simple and effective ways to display a variety of data types.

Why Use It:

- To show *relative* magnitude
- To show *trends*
- To show *changes* between trends
- To provide a visual comparison of process *performance* to customer *requirements*

When:

- During presentations that require clarity with quantitative impact
- To combine with pie charts and line graphs in a presentation or document to add variety as well as providing a quantitative emphasis
- Whenever increments between measurements are useful, or important, to see clearly
- Whenever year-to-year (multiply years, or time periods) comparisons must be clear

Do not attempt to do a thing unless you are sure of yourself; but do not relinquish it simply because someone else is not sure of you.
--Stewart E. White

<u>*QUICK VIEW*</u>

<u>**BAR CHART**</u>

AVERAGE NUMBER OF VISITS A PERSON
MAKES TO A PHYSICIAN EACH YEAR

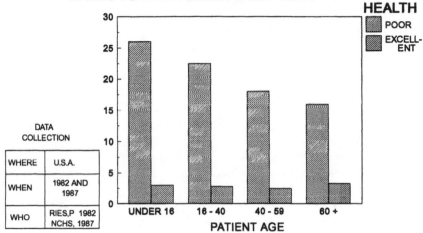

DATA COLLECTION	
WHERE	U.S.A.
WHEN	1982 AND 1987
WHO	RIES,P 1982 NCHS, 1987

<u>*NOTES*</u>

1. Collect data.

2. Determine categories; each one will be a bar.

3. Determine the category with highest value. Use that value to establish the Y axis highest value.

4. Label the X axis and the Y axis.

5. Construct the bars.

My Ideas and Items to practice at the next team meeting

Achieve these Potentials

NOTES

....

....

....

....

....

....

POTENTIALS	ACHIEVING POTENTIALS
Simple, but effective data display	The old motto is, "if in doubt, make a bar chart." Most people don't say that old motto, they simply do it. And, no wonder. Why question success. Bar charts become a successful habit. They can be vertical, horizontal, independent bars, stacked bars, simple or multiple data sets, and three-dimensional.
Independent Bars	Independent bars can be used with multiple data sets. In the example in Figure A, the number of beach closings is shown for each coastal county of a certain state over a four-year period. There is one data set for each county and *independent* bars by county and year.

SEE FIGURE A

Stacked Bars	By stacking bars on top of bars, we can examine more data. Figure B shows the same beach closing data as Figure A, but the cause of the closing is shown for each coastal county A, B, and C, by year.

Multiple data sets like this become confusing for display on bar charts, and thereby confusing to the team. The 3-D bar chart and the line chart (next chapter) can help greatly. |

SEE FIGURE B

My Ideas and Items to practice at the next team meeting

....

....

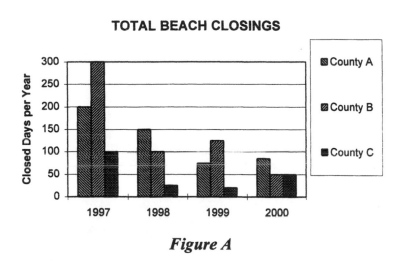

Figure A

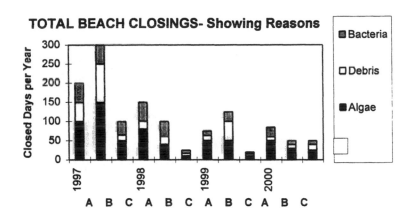

A,B, and C are counties on the coast of a North Atlantic
state in this example, which is based on an actual case.

Figure B

My Ideas and Items to practice at the next team meeting

NOTES

Achieve these Potentials

NOTES

....

....

....

....

....

....

....

POTENTIALS	ACHIEVING POTENTIALS
3-D Bars	By using three dimensions, we can separate the data to create a different, and sometimes more effective, picture:

TOTAL BEACH CLOSINGS - Showing Reasons

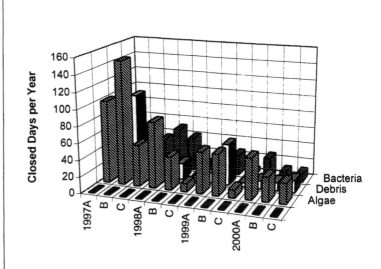

A,B, and C are counties on the coast of a North Atlantic state in this example, which is based on an actual case.

My Ideas and Items to practice at the next team meeting

....

....

PITFALLS	AVOIDING PITFALLS
Over used. Pie Charts or Line Charts may display the data and issues better	Try another type of chart. First make a sketch of the chart. Ask yourself what message that sketch carries, and what information it provides or does not provide. Try another sketch of another chart. Decide which is best. You may want to use both.
Bar Charts can be confusing when displaying four or more data sets over time	The following data display begins to be confusing:

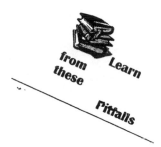

ORDER AND BILLING PROCESSES

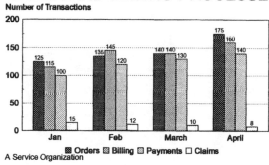

A three-dimensional chart can help because the monthly trends are easier to track:

ORDER AND BILLING PROCESSES
Number of Transactions

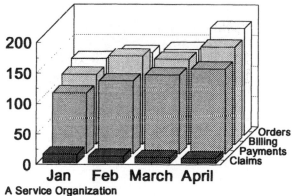

My Ideas and Items to practice at the next team meeting

NOTES

....

....

....

....

....

....

PITFALLS	AVOIDING PITFALLS
Bar charts can be confusing when displaying four or more data sets over time (Continued)	Also, a line chart can create an effective separation of the data sets, and is generally the recommended chart for four or more data sets:

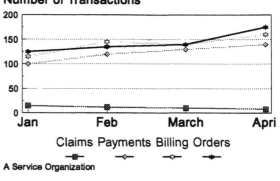

My Ideas and Items to practice at the next team meeting

....

....

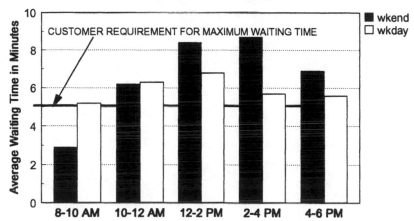

AVERAGE CUSTOMER WAITING TIME
BY TIME OF DAY

(Chart shows bars for wkend and wkday across time periods; Y-axis "Average Waiting Time in Minutes" from 0 to 10; horizontal line labeled "CUSTOMER REQUIREMENT FOR MAXIMUM WAITING TIME"; X-axis categories: 8-10 AM, 10-12 AM, 12-2 PM, 2-4 PM, 4-6 PM)

MANUAL SKETCH, OR COMPUTER GENERATION, OR BOTH

Computer graphic programs today can usually construct a bar chart automatically. There are reasons the construction steps that follow can be useful *even if you have a graphics program.* See this discussion under pie charts, the points are the same.

HOW TO CONSTRUCT A BAR CHART

1. Collect data on the subject. A check sheet is one way to collect such data when counting events is involved. Besides frequency, bar charts can show dollars, volume, weight, percentages, and virtually any other measure.

2. Make a table displaying the data, as in this example:

My Ideas and Items to practice at the next team meeting

NOTES

Average Customer Waiting Time (minutes)*

	8-10 AM	10-12	1-2 PM	2-4 PM	4-6 PM
Weekend	2.9	6.2	8.4	8.7	6.9
Weekday	5.2	6.3	6.8	5.7	5.6

*Ten customers randomly selected during each interval of the day.

3. Create an X-Y frame, with Y as the vertical axis. This Y-axis will display the measurements, i.e., the collected data. In this example, the X-axis will show when the data occurred.

4. Find the largest data point among the measurements and use it to determine the range on the Y-axis, which usually goes from zero to the largest measurement, or a convenient value beyond the largest measurement. Then divide the Y-axis into segments, usually units of 1, or 2, or 5, or 10, or 50, etc.

5. Construct the bar in the X-Y frame; one bar for each measurement.

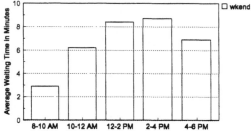

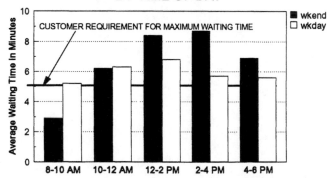

My Ideas and Items to practice at the next team meeting

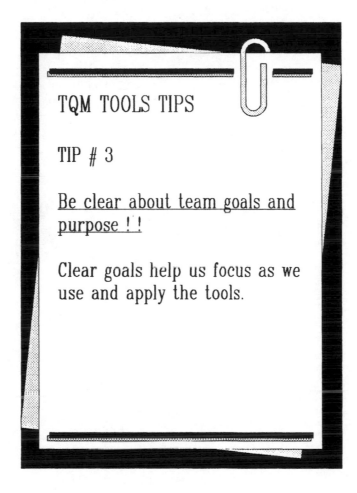

TQM TOOLS TIPS

TIP # 3

Be clear about team goals and
purpose ! !

Clear goals help us focus as we
use and apply the tools.

The farther back you can look, the farther forward you are likely to see.

Winston Churchill

9

SITUATION:

Team Members Say -

"Let's see the trend of this data over time."

"I want to see if there are patterns over time."

"Here are three responses from each of 100 people we interviewed. It is is not data over time, but I want to see the pattern over these 100 interviewees."

"We have several sets of data here and bar charts are confusing with this much data. What should we use?"

SOLUTION:

Line Chart (Also called Run Chart or Trend Chart)

Let us, then, be up and doing,
  With a heart for any fate;
Still achieving, still pursuing,
  Learn to labor and to wait.
--Henry Wadsworth Longfellow

Line Chart

What Is It:

A line - it can be straight or wavy - showing the change, usually over time, of a variable that is being measured within the process. When the change is shown over time, such as hours or days, the name "run" or "trend" chart applies. "Line chart" is the general name that applies.

Why Use It:

- To display *sequential* measurements from a process
- To display *trends,* such as upward or downward slides
- To display *patterns,* such as cycles and periodic outlines
- To provide a visual comparison of *process performance* to Customer Requirements
- To provide a visual display of the *variation* in process performance over time
- To *compare* the pattern of one data set with another

When:

- Anytime data needs to be displayed in sequence to facilitate understanding and decisions about trends, changes, and variations
- Before and after an improvement in the process
- When looking for irregularities in process performance

Life affords no higher pleasure than that of
surmounting difficulties, passing from one step of
success to another, forming new wishes and seeing
them gratified.
--Samuel Johnson

QUICK VIEW

LINE CHART

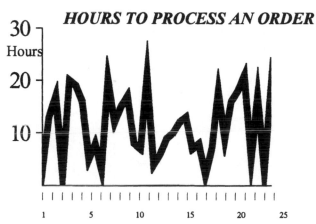

HOURS TO PROCESS AN ORDER

DATA
COLLECTION

ORDER NUMBER

WHERE: AMES PLANT
WHEN: OCTOBER
WHO: ORDER HANDLING TEAM

1. Collect data.

2. Determine the time intervals or the sequence numbers for the X axis (the horizontal axis).

3. Determine the highest value of the data. Use that value to establish the highest scale value for the Y axis.

4. Label the X and Y axis.

5. Plot the data points and costruct the line chart.

My Ideas and Items to practice at the next team meeting

POTENTIALS	ACHIEVING POTENTIALS
Trends or patterns can be compared to business objectives or Customer Requirements	Plot the data in sequential fashion on the line chart. Then draw a horizontal line, or a band of two lines, that represents the desired level of the customers, or of those managing the process. Look for data points, patterns, or trends that are outside of requirements. Consider improving the process to correct the output.
Multiple data sets can be plotted for comparison	A primary advantage of a line chart over bar charts is the ability to clearly show multiple data sets. It is the chart of choice for three or more sets of data shown on one chart.

Achieve these Potentials

NOTES

....

....

....

....

....

....

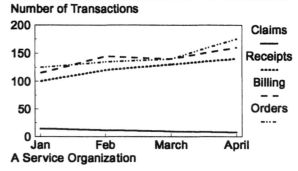

ORDER AND BILLING PROCESSES
Number of Transactions

Patterns - by particular hour, or certain day of the week, etc. - can provide clues to special causes of process variation	Look for patterns. Consider them as learning areas. Why does the process do consistently better (or perhaps poorer) on Monday of each week, for example. Use other tools to explore the issue, like cause/effect diagram, and further data collection and display.
See "Process Variation" later in this chapter	

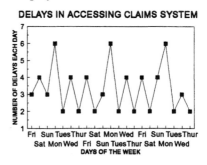

My Ideas and Items to practice at the next team meeting

....

....

PITFALLS	AVOIDING PITFALLS
Samples may be biased	Line charts are often used to study trends or patterns. Sometimes excessive amounts of data are generated by the process we are studying. When large amounts of data are available each day from a process, we often select a fixed-size sample each day, or each hour, for example. We might choose, for example, five data points each day for a month out of many hundreds of data points. Sampling is used to reduce the volume of the data and thereby reduce the effort in collecting and analyzing it. *But samples can lead to biases.* Avoid taking all samples in the same hour if the sample is intended to represent the whole day. Avoid taking all samples at one work station if it is to represent them all. Select each sample data point in a random fashion.
Data may be scarce	*Opposite of excessive data, that leads to sampling, is scarce data.* Line charts are often used to study trends and patterns, but scarce data renders such trends or patterns sketchy and unreliable. As a general rule, collect at least 20 data points before looking for a trend, and even then, be aware that the line chart patterns may be misleading. Thirty data points is better, 50 is truly acceptable, and 100 is generally delightful.
Manual tracking effort may be time consuming	If large volumes of data exist, and you need to collect samples, or even if you choose to plot all of the data, a mechanized means of collecting and even displaying the data might be wise to consider. Plan ahead.
A trend that moves in the desired direction may not be a good sign	Improvements in process outputs can occur from extra inspection, extra rework, and other *added non-conformance costs.* We want outputs to improve with increased planning, decreased inspection, and decreased waste and rework. Whatever trend occurs in your process, investigate to discovery why it is occurring.

from Learn *these* Pitfalls

NOTES

....

....

....

....

....

....

My Ideas and Items to practice at the next team meeting

....

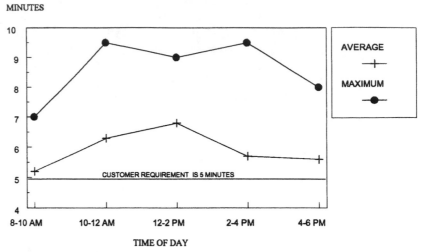

WEEKDAY CUSTOMER WAITING TIME

DATA COLLECT BY THE PROCESS IMPROVEMENT

TEAM, FEB-MARCH, AT MAIN STORE

NOTES

MANUAL SKETCH, OR COMPUTER GENERATION, OR BOTH?

As with pie and bar charts, line graphs can also be automatically constructed by a computer graphics program. But there are reasons to sketch them by hand *even if such a software package is available.* See the discussion under pie charts.

HOW TO CONSTRUCT A LINE GRAPH

1. Collect data on the subject. You may have multiple data sets, that is, one set of data for each of three years (therefore three data sets), or a different set of data for different geographic areas, etc.

My Ideas and Items to practice at the next team meeting

Customer Waiting Time (Minutes)

Weekend	8-10 AM	10-12	12-2 PM	2-4 PM	4-6 PM
Average	2.9	6.2	8.4	8.7	6.9
Maximum	5.0	13.0	11.5	15.0	12.0
Weekday					
Average	5.2	6.3	6.8	5.7	5.6
Maximum	7.0	9.5	9.0	9.5	8.0

2. Construct the X-Y frame. The Y-axis will be the vertical one and will display the measurements, i.e., the actual data values. The X-axis will show 'when', or time of day, in this example.

3. Determine the largest data value in your sets of data and use it to create the scale on the Y-axis. It is often useful to select the highest scale value as 1.25 or 1.5 times the highest data point value. Divide the Y-axis into increments. Small increments allow small changes to be seen in the graph, but the Y-axis may become quite long. A balance is needed. Experiment with increments of 1, 5, 10, 50, etc.

4. Place the intervals on the X axis. Often this is time, such as years, or months, or weeks, or hours, etc. Use equally spaced intervals.

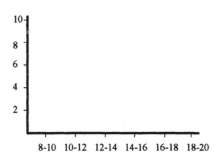

5. Plot the data points. If you have multiple data sets, plot one full set, then start another.

6. Use different line patterns or colors to show different data set trend lines. Label each.

7. Show a data collection box: Who collected the data, where, when.

My Ideas and Items to practice at the next team meeting

The line chart below shows waiting times in a customer service line at a store. Because hundreds of customers wait in line each day, samples were taken. Ten samples - not shown here - were taken for each time period (8 AM - 10 AM, 10 AM - 12 Noon, etc.) each day for 20 days. This gave 200 samples for each time period.

The average of these samples are shown on the line chart. Those averages give a slight curved line that might suggest that waiting times are not far from the customer required time of five minutes or less. But averages can be misleading. The maximum waiting times suggest that the spread of the data is large and that there are many customers experiencing a significantly long waiting time.

NOTES

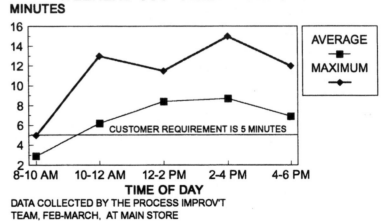

WEEKEND CUSTOMER WAITING TIME

DATA COLLECTED BY THE PROCESS IMPROV'T
TEAM, FEB-MARCH, AT MAIN STORE

My Ideas and Items to practice at the next team meeting

PROCESS VARIATION

All processes have variation. Measurements taken at any point inside a process, or at the output of a process will show variation over time. Variation is natural. Further, a process that is operating with no external or internal special effects, or special forces, or biases, will have a variation that is 'random'. The measurements will be randomly varying up and down around the average. The randomness of the variation means, for example, that you will not be able to predict the next data point before it is actually measured. It could be anywhere. With a 'non-random' process, we can generally guess roughly where the next point will lie because of some pattern that we see on the line chart, as discussed later in this section.

Variation, then is natural. We want, however, to keep that variation within the limits of the customer specifications. In addition, we may have placed specifications on the process ourselves, and we want the measures to remain within our specifications either for safety, or cost containment, or other reasons.

Line Charts are very useful for displaying the variations and for allowing clear comparison to specifications. By making the performance visible relative to specifications, we can have both a sense of the degree of improvement needed, and an actual physical measure of the gap between performance and specifications.

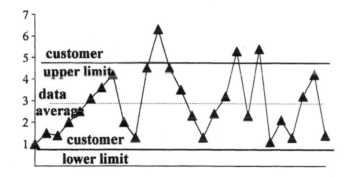

In the above line chart, or run chart, the process is satisfying the customer requirements on average. Someone could say, " Our process is satisfying requirements well. It is performing at about 3 units which is right in the middle of the upper and lower customer specifications." We can see, however, that in three cases the process was out of limits, and it runs very close to the upper and lower limits most of the time. The chapter on Histograms discusses the desirability to reduce the variation of our process measurements, and this is one such example. Averages are generally not very useful, we

NOTES

My Ideas and Items to practice at the next team meeting

must instead look at the swings and variations that occur. Further, we must be certain that those swings do not cross the specification limits set by ourselves or our customers.

Line charts also reveal statistical abnormalities in processes. A process may be satisfying customer requirements and be fully within the specification limits, yet be behaving in 'abnormal' or 'non-random' fashion. Line charts combined with what are called 'run tests' can reveal those abnormal situations. The value of discovering them is that we can improve the process, thereby reducing costs, frustration, rework, and the like. In other words, by uncovering any non-random behavior in our process, we can work to remove the biases and other events that are causing that non-randomness, and thereby have a process that runs smoother and very often with less swings or variation. Suppose, for example, that you drive to work each day, and that you choose to record the travel time each morning. Let us further suppose that you set an upper limit of 30 minutes for the drive, which you hope to be able to meet by arranging your departure time, and the route you take. Perhaps this is the resultant line chart:

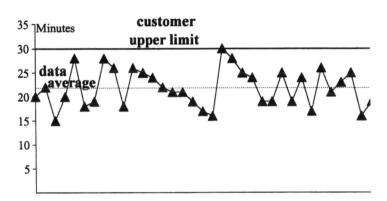

At first glance we might be fairly pleased with the results. The variation is between 15 and 30 minutes, which is not excellent, but acceptable, at least for a start. The average is about 22 minutes, and the maximum is usually around 25 on the most recent drives. On second glance, however, this process does not appear to be operating in a purely random fashion. Some forces are apparently at work that are causing it to have patterns in its performance. The indicators are all statistical, so we cannot say for certain that the process is free of special effects, but we can say that the probability that the patterns that are happening would happen by chance, or accidentally, is about 1 out of 750.

My Ideas and Items to practice at the next team meeting

NOTES

Three 'run tests' can be applied to line charts or run charts:

○ Nine data points in a row on the same side of the average.
○ Six data points in a row that have a continuous rising or falling pattern.
○ A periodic pattern that resembles a wave, or a saw-toothed pattern. Two examples are shown below.

Examples of Periodic Patterns that imply
an abnormal condition in a process:

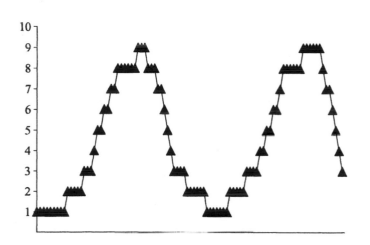

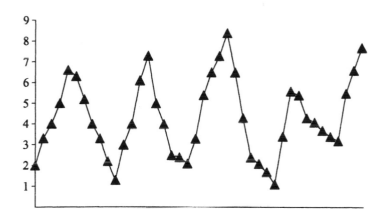

My Ideas and Items to practice at the next team meeting

For our drive to work, the line chart passes run tests #1 and #3, but not #2. We see from the line chart that more than seven consecutive data points have a falling pattern. The implication is that we can perhaps find the cause of that pattern, and improve the process. In this case, the downward trend was desirable, so our objective would most likely be not to eliminate the cause of that pattern, but to find the cause and try to build it into the process! If, for example, the decrease came from leaving earlier and earlier each successive morning, we might want to build that into the process.

In summary, variations are normal, but we strive to keep those variations within specified limits, and to look for abnormalities in those variations that can be a strong clue on ways to improve the process.

NOTES

....

....

....

....

....

....

....

My Ideas and Items to practice at the next team meeting

....

....

The mode by which the inevitable comes to pass is effort.
--Oliver Wendell Holmes

The greatest difficulties lie where we are not looking for them.

Johann von Goethe
Philosopher and novelist
1749 -1832

10

SITUATION:

Team Members Say -

"Where do we focus?"

"Let's display the vital few - those few items that are causing most of the difficulty."

"I've heard about the 80/20 rule - where 80 percent of the errors are caused by only 20 percent of all the types of failures. How can we display that?"

SOLUTION:

Pareto Chart

From principles is derived probability, but truth or certainty is obtained only from facts.
--Nathaniel Hawthorne

Pareto Diagram

What Is It:

A bar chart in descending order, showing a frequency measure for each of several events, to allow relative comparison.

Why Use It:

- To have a picture showing one of several frequenicies:
    - Number of *occurrences*
    - Amount of *time* for each item
    - Amount of *resources* needed for each item
    - *Impact* of each on customer
    - Other measures

- To *separate* "Vital Few" from "Useful Many," as a start to making a decision on how to proceed with improving the process under study. (These terms are credited to Dr. J. Juran).
- To have a graphical display of *performance* that can be compared with Customer Requirements.

When:

- Valuable for understanding relative frequency of errors
- Often useful during any data oriented step of Process Improvement
- Can be useful in selecting which process to address, by charting, for example, complaints for each process
- Useful in evaluating progress of an improved operation in the process; comparing an old chart to a new one

The wind and the waves are always on the side of the ablest navigators.
--Edward Gibbon

QUICK VIEW

<u>PARETO CHART</u>

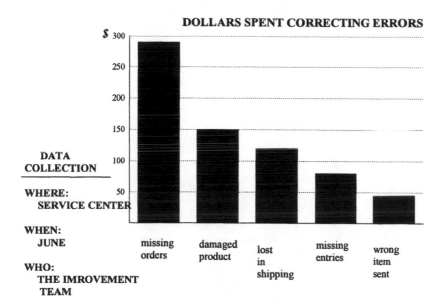

**DATA
COLLECTION**

**WHERE:
SERVICE CENTER**

**WHEN:
JUNE**

**WHO:
THE IMROVEMENT
TEAM**

1. Establish the types of errors or categories of events to explore within the process.

2. Collect data by error type or by event.

3. Place the data in decending order. The error type or category with the highest data value - the highest frequency - is placed first in this decending list.

4. Place a scale on thc vertical, or Y, axis.

5. Place the error types or events on the X Axis and plot the vertical bars.

My Ideas and Items to practice at the next team meeting

POTENTIALS	ACHIEVING POTENTIALS
We find one or two events that are out-standing on the Pareto Diagram in terms of (1)Customer Impact, and (2)Ease of correction	We are looking for the event, or type of error, or particular category that is not only the largest in frequency, but which has the largest impact on customers and is the least expensive to rectify. In other words, the benefit-to-cost ratio is high. Remember that high customer impact does not necessarily equate to high frequency. An error can happen often but simply be a minor impact on your customer. Another type of error may be infrequent but debilitating to your customer's own process. *The key is to measure or estimate customer impact.* Figure A on the next page shows the frequency of billing errors for a certain utility company. These errors occurred in 10,000 bills issued by the company. Errors in the amount of the bill were *most frequent* by far. The team might consider fixing that error first, until Figure B is considered. There we see that the big *impact on the customer is in correcting the error* when the wrong service is shown on the bill. In this case, the customer impact was estimated by contacting all customers that had an error on their bill and asking for the number of hours and number of employees involved (if it was a business customer) in correcting the bill. Sometimes computer systems of the customer were also involved and the time and cost of those were considered. Employee hours and computer hours were then converted to dollars. In addition, Figure C shows the relative cost to the utility itself.
The *Pareto Categories* may be useful on a *Cause/Effect Diagram*	Cause and Effect Diagrams can have generic categories, as discussed in Chapter 13. But the categories from a Pareto Diagram can be useful in further exploring the causes of poor system performance. For example, to further explore difficulties in the billing system, we can use, from the previous example "amount, dates, address, and services rendered" as the main categories on a C/E Diagram. This is often a useful way to explore a process deeper.
A simple yet effective way to display daily information and begin to see possibilities	When we have little to guide our improvement efforts, Pareto Diagrams provide a visible picture of the relative frequency of events that stimulates exploration of the other avenues and collection of other sets of data. Simply plot your data. Try it. See where it takes you.

Achieve these Potentials

NOTES

....

....

....

....

....

....

My Ideas and Items to practice at the next team meeting

....

....

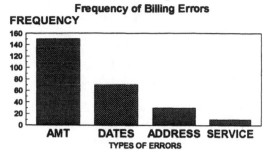

Pareto Diagram
Frequency of Billing Errors

FREQUENCY

Figure A

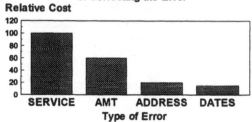

Pareto Diagram
**Relative Cost to Customer
of Correcting the Error**

Relative Cost

Figure B

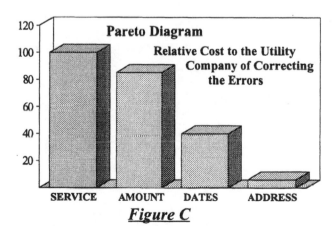

Figure C

My Ideas and Items to practice at the next team meeting

Learn from these Pitfalls

NOTES

PITFALLS	AVOIDING PITFALLS
Data displays a uniform Pareto - no outstanding items	It often happens: You collect some data, make a Pareto diagram, and the bars are nearly all the same height. There is no indication from that diagram on where to begin further exploration. The solution is to remember that data has many facets. Try another view of the data; in fact, try several. See the example at the end of this section.
Belief that the Pareto Diagram automatically determines the problems/ events to pursue	The highest bar on a Pareto Diagram is not necessarily the place to begin process improvement activities. The benefit/cost ratio needs to be addressed. The key tool to use after a Pareto Diagram is often a *Decision Matrix* where the criteria are selected, such as customer impact, cost to rectify, savings if corrected, and feasibility. Those criteria are then used along with the Pareto Diagram data and other data to select which of the error types, events, or categories to address. See Chapter 14 on the Decision Matrix for more detail.
Sufficient data has not been taken to be accurate about a decision	We often need to ask questions about possibilities and about other data needed before proceeding. A common trait of teams is to jump to a solution. A useful philosophy is to remember that questions and explanations are sometimes more important than seeking quick solutions. Exploration means collecting facts, data, information, and ideas about other types of data that can be useful.

My Ideas and Items to practice at the next team meeting

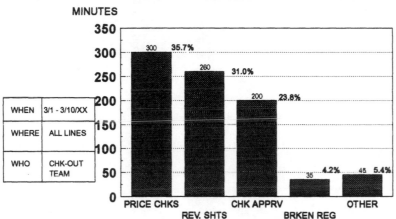

PARETO DIAGRAM OF TIME TAKEN DURING SELECTED
ACTIVITIES OF THE CUSTOMER PAYMENTS PROCESS

WHEN	3/1 - 3/10/XX
WHERE	ALL LINES
WHO	CHK-OUT TEAM

NOTES

HOW TO CONSTRUCT A PARETO DIAGRAM

1. Identify the problem area to be analyzed.

2. Determine the types of errors, or the categories of events, on which you will collect data. Sometimes it helps to collect data first to know what the categories are.

3. Collect data on each category or type of error.

Check Approval	200 minutes
Price Checks	300 minutes
Using Review Sheets	260 minutes
Broken Cash Register	35 minutes
Other	45 minutes

My Ideas and Items to practice at the next team meeting

4. List Categories in descending order.

Price Checks	300 minutes
Using Review Sheets	260 minutes
Check Approval	200 minutes
Broken Cash Register	35 minutes
Other	45 minutes

5. Construct an X-Y frame and determine the scale on the Y-axis based on the largest data point. Choose units for the Y-axis just as described in the section on bar charts. Label the Y-axis.

6. The X-axis of a Pareto Diagram always contains the categories. The category on the far left side of the X-axis is the one with the highest, or largest, data point.

7. Construct the vertical bars. Construct the data box showing who collected the data, when, and where.

NOTES

8. You can also place percentages on a Pareto Diagram. To calculate the percentage that is associated with each bar, divide the height of each bar (the data point for each bar) by the sum of all the data points.

9. Each category (each bar) on a Pareto Diagram can perhaps be broken down further, into subcategories.

Example: The Pareto Diagram on the previous page results from the data in Item 4 above. Price checks take a long time. If we examine time doing price checks by type of packaging, we have this Pareto Diagram:

**PARETO DIAGRAM OF TIME SPENT ON PRICE CHECKS
BY CATEGORY OF PACKAGING**

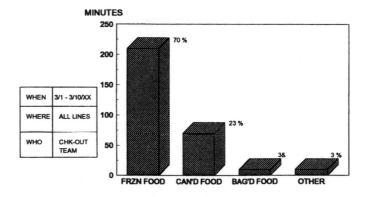

My Ideas and Items to practice at the next team meeting

☑   *Tip:*   **One set** *of data may be able to be* **expanded to several sets** *of data, and that may help in generating an informative Pareto Diagram. For example, you may have one set of data, such as number of errors by type. But you may be able to extract from that single set of data:*

Number of errors by day of the week.
Number of errors by geographic location.
Number of errors by type of equipment involved.
Number of errors by morning, day, evening shift.
Number of errors by location in the process, etc.

By plotting different Pareto charts you may find one that shows a pattern of a high error rate by day, or by geographic location, etc.

Example:

Errors in Order Process

Item #	Type Error	Location	Time Period
1	Wrong Form	Western	AM
2	Wrong Form	Eastern	Afternoon
3	Wrong Form	Eastern	PM
4	Wrong Form	Eastern	PM
5	Wrong Inventory #	Southern	Afternoon
6	Wrong Inventory #	Eastern	AM
7	Wrong Inventory #	Central	AM
8	Missing Data	Eastern	PM
9	Missing Data	Central	Afternoon
10	Missing Data	Eastern	AM
11	Missing Data	Eastern	PM
12	Missing Data	Western	Afternoon
13	Missing Data	Eastern	AM

The Pareto Charts for this data are on the next page.

My Ideas and Items to practice at the next team meeting

Pareto Diagram
By Type of Error

Frequency

MD	WF	WI

Type of Error

NOTES

....

....

....

....

....

....

Pareto Diagram
By Location

Frequency

EASTERN	WESTERN	CENTRAL	SOUTHERN

Location

Pareto Diagram
By Time of Day

Frequency

AM	AFTERNOON	PM

Time of Day

My Ideas and Items to practice at the next team meeting

....

....

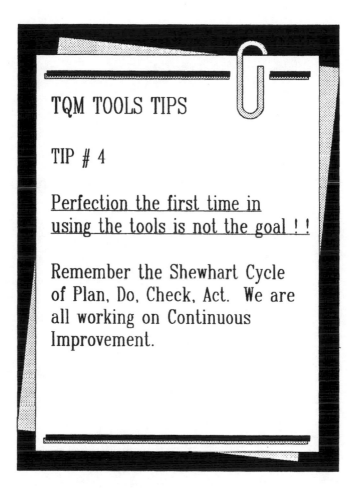

TQM TOOLS TIPS

TIP # 4

Perfection the first time in
using the tools is not the goal ! !

Remember the Shewhart Cycle
of Plan, Do, Check, Act. We are
all working on Continuous
Improvement.

It takes less time to do a thing right than it does to explain
why you did it wrong

Henry Wadsworth Longfellow

SITUATION:

Team Members Say -

"We have many data points on the process - do we simply calculate an average?"

"An average seems misleading to me - sometimes a measurement was small, other times large."

"How can we see all the data at one time?"

"Right, I want a picture of all the data."

"Can we see where Customer Requirements fit on that picture?"

SOLUTION:

Histogram

The question "Who ought to be boss?" is like asking
"Who ought to be the tenor in the quartet?"
Obviously, the person who can sing tenor.
--Henry Ford

Histogram

What Is It:

A graphical display of the frequency of measurements that fall within specified intervals. It shows the distribution of the data, that is, what measurement occurs most often, least often, etc.

Why Use It:

- To show the frequency distribution, or *shape,* of a set of data
- To show the variance, or *spread,* of that data
- To provide a *visual display* of a process output compared to Customer's Requirements
- To provide a *snapshot* in time

When:

- Useful during planning, checking and other data collection steps (see PDCA in the Preface)
- Anytime a set of measurements needs to be analyzed for range, spread, and distribution as a snapshot in time
- Displaying the capability of the process compared to requirements on it
- Forming a visual profile of the current performance of a process that can later be compared to an improved performance profile

In this world there is always danger for those who are afraid of it.
--George Bernard Shaw

HISTOGRAM
TIME WAITING FOR SERVICE

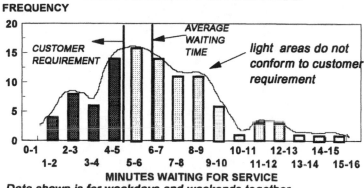

Data shown is for weekdays and weekends together

1. Collect the data and list it in ascending order.

2. Decide on the number of intervals to have on the horizontal axis.

3. Determine the width of each interval.

4. Determine the starting point on the horizontal axis for the first interval. The other intervals automatically fall in place.

5. Count the number of measurements from No. 1 above that fall in each interval. If a data point falls right on the line separating two intervals, simply decide if you want it in the left interval or the right. See step 7 on page 167 for details.

6. Construct a vertical bar of the count in No. 5 above.

My Ideas and Items to practice at the next team meeting

NOTES

....

....

....

....

....

....

POTENTIALS	ACHIEVING POTENTIALS
A distribution of the data results that is expected, such as a bell shaped (or Normal) curve. The team would then address narrowing or shifting the curve, as needed	The most common shape for a Histogram is a so-called bell shape. It often occurs in nature, such as with the heights of people, the number of centimeters between leaves on a tree, or the percent of some gas, like carbon dioxide, measured in the air each day. Each of these measurements is taken for an outcome or event that is random and not totally predictable. Heights vary. Temperatures vary. The first mathematician to describe this bell shape was Gauss, and he called it a *Normal shape because of the natural tendency for it to occur.*

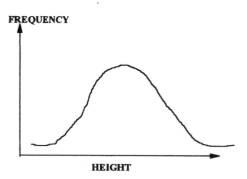

But a Normal curve may not be the expected result for measurements from your process. You may expect a skewed distribution - one that leans to one side.

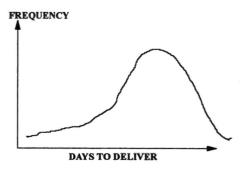

My Ideas and Items to practice at the next team meeting

....

....

POTENTIALS	ACHIEVING POTENTIALS

A skewed shape can result when an upper or lower limit exists, such as a policy that no delivery exceeds 20 days.

Whatever the natural shape is for your process, the next step is to *better satisfy customer requirements,* and to render the process more efficient. Faster delivery time would result in the above histogram shifting to the left. More predictable delivery time would be displayed by the histogram being narrower. Process improvement activities can affect *both.*

A distribution results that is unexpected, such as a bimodal distribution when a bell shape was expected - the team would address that as a potential for Process Improvement

Unexpected histogram shapes mean opportunities to find causes and to improve the process. If you expect a Normal shape, but a Bimodal one occurs, there is an opportunity to bring efficiencies into the process.

NOTES

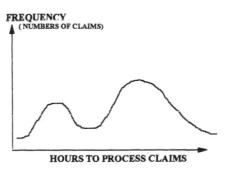

FREQUENCY
(NUMBERS OF CLAIMS)

HOURS TO PROCESS CLAIMS

The Bimodal shape may be due to different work groups, one well skilled, the other not yet; or due to different types of items (claims, in the above chart) being handled, some complex and some simple. Investigation of the cause will allow a reduction of the less satisfactory peak and a narrowing of the entire curve.

....

....

....

....

....

....

My Ideas and Items to practice at the next team meeting

....

POTENTIALS	ACHIEVING POTENTIALS
The gap between Customer Requirements, or other specifications on the process, and performance can be seen. The size of the gap is visible	Your process may be satisfying your customer on average, but failing a significant portion of the time. A *histogram will quantify* the amount and degree of failure

Achieve these **Potentials**

NOTES

....

....

....

....

....

....

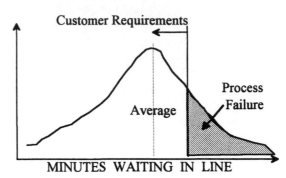

to meet customer requirements. To satisfy the customer, in the above chart, all of the histogram must be to the left of the requirement line. The fact that the <u>average</u> performance is "satisfactory" is of little consequence. This simple but powerful chart shows us how much we have to shift and narrow the output distribution if we are to satisfy - and perhaps retain - our customers.

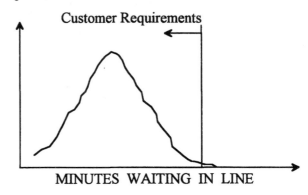

My Ideas and Items to practice at the next team meeting

....

....

PITFALLS	AVOIDING PITFALLS
Insufficient data to form a reliable distribution	Some processes, especially in service oriented companies, produce outputs infrequently. Data from such processes can be scarce. Weeks or months can occur before 50 data points are available. Constructing a histogram with less than 50 data points can led to misinterpretations because the shape is incomplete. To avoid misjudgment, attempt to have at least 50 data points. If only 20 or 30 points are available, certainly use and display them. A shape or a pattern may become clear. *Simply be cautious in making decisions with less than 50 data points.* Continue to collect data.
Large volume of data, causing the team to wonder how to cope with it	Some processes generate hundreds of data points a day. Sampling the data is an effective way to obtain a representative histogram without using all the data. Sampling is done randomly. If there are 100 transactions each day, and we measure the time to complete each one, a random sample would be accomplished by selecting data points at random across the day. We would not select every fifth data point, or take all of them in the morning, for example. Another approach to handling large volumes of data is to use a personal computer software program to generate the distribution, but this often requires manual entry of data into the software. Again, sampling is useful.
Pareto Charts are sometimes mistaken for Histograms	Pareto charts always have events - like types of errors, or department names, etc. - on the horizontal axis. There are always *words*, or code numbers ("error type 1") on the horizontal axis. Histograms always have measurements on the horizontal axis - like delivery time in minutes, or height in inches. Also, a Pareto chart is always constructed with the highest frequency to the left, then the next highest, etc. The vertical bars are placed in descending order. For a histogram, the measurement data is counted for each interval and it results in a vertical bar. That bar is with one particular measurement interval on the horizontal axis and cannot be arbitrarily shifted left or right.

from these Learn

Pitfalls

NOTES

....

....

....

....

....

....

My Ideas and Items to practice at the next team meeting

....

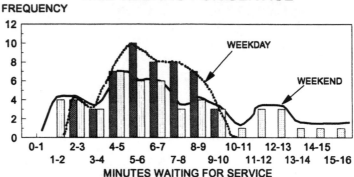

HISTOGRAM
TIME WAITING FOR SERVICE

Separate data for weekdays and weekends

HOW TO CONSTRUCT A HISTOGRAM

1. A Histogram shows a measurement on the X-axis, and that measurement is divided into intervals, as we will see.

    First, decide what measurement you want to take. Often you can plan this by visualizing one item flowing through your process (through the column flow chart description of the process, for example) and deciding what you want to measure on that item. Typical measurements of items traveling through a process are:

    - Time to travel between two points
    - Time waiting in a queue
    - Weight
    - Length, or size
    - Dollar value (such as for an insurance claim, or a manufactured piece)
    - Complexity (number of data fields, pages, etc.)
    - Number of items passing through the process in an hour (or day)
    - Number of times each item flowing through a process 'bounces' inside the process because errors occur that need to be corrected.

My Ideas and Items to practice at the next team meeting

2. Collect and record the data. Try to have at least 50 data points because the shape of the Histogram is a more accurate representation of the distribution of the data the more sample data points you have. If you only have 30 data points, then proceed with the Histogram, but be careful in making decisions around the shape of the Histogram.

3. Place the data in ascending order.

4. Compute the range; the difference between the highest and the smallest data points. The X-axis of the Histogram must, and will, cover this range. Label the range 'R'.

5. The number of intervals needed on the X-axis can be computed by $\sqrt{N}$ where N is the number of data points, and $\sqrt{N}$ is the square root of N. This is only a guide.

6. The width of each of these intervals will be $R/\sqrt{N}$, which means dividing the range by the square root of the number of data points. This may sound complicated, but it is simply a way to be certain that the histogram will cover the whole range of the data as the intervals (all $\sqrt{N}$ of them) span the horizontal (X) axis.

7. We now have the width of each interval and the number of them. All we need for the X-axis now is a starting point. The starting point can simply be picked as the lowest data point (lowest measurement). Alternatively (not shown on the graphs here), we can define the starting point as the lowest data point minus one-half a measurement unit. This one-half unit is subtracted to prevent confusion over which interval a data point goes into if it falls right on the break line between two intervals. By subtracting one-half a unit, no data point can fall on a tic mark on the horizontal axis. If you chose not to subtract one-half a unit, simply assign those data points that fall directly on the line between intervals (the 'tic' marks that mark the intervals) to either the left or the right interval.

8. **Count the number of measurements that fall in each interval. <u>Example:</u>**

<u>A</u> Interval Number	<u>B</u> Interval Limit	<u>C</u> Number of Data Points in Each Interval
1	0 - 1 minutes	0
2	1 - 2 minutes	4
3	2 - 3 minutes	8
4	3 - 4 minutes	6
5	4 - 5 minutes	14
6	5 - 6 minutes	17

NOTES

....

....

....

....

....

....

My Ideas and Items to practice at the next team meeting

....

....

9. Construct an X-Y frame with the Y-axis scale covering the highest number in column C above. The X-axis shows intervals from steps 4-7 here.

10. Label both the X axis and the Y axis. The Y axis can always be labeled "frequency". You may choose to label the Y axis with a descriptor that applies to the particular data study being conducted. For the table of data above, for example, where the number of people waiting in line is being studied by how long they wait, we could use "Number of Customers Waiting in Line" as the label for the Y axis.

    The label for the X axis is always a description of the measurement intervals that are there on the X axis. In the example above this would be "Minutes", or we could say "Minutes Customers Wait in Line".

11. Construct the vertical bars on the X-Y frame. Then draw a smooth line connecting the tops of the bars simply as a way of making the shape of the distribution more apparent.

NOTES

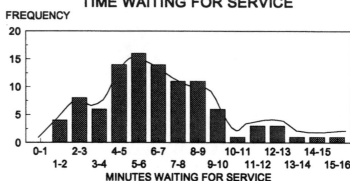

HISTOGRAM
TIME WAITING FOR SERVICE

Data shown is for weekdays and weekends together

12. Now you are ready to explore the data further, if you choose. In the above example, both weekday and weekend data are shown together. But customers visiting the store may experience different waiting times on weekends than on weekdays. Separating the data to show two histograms may help us decide what to do first to decrease customer waiting time. **The histogram on the next page shows the separate data sets.**

My Ideas and Items to practice at the next team meeting

HISTOGRAM
TIME WAITING FOR SERVICE

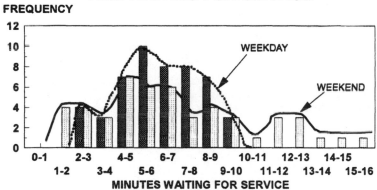

Separate data for weekdays and weekends

This histogram shows that weekend customers experience a wider range of times waiting in line than do weekday customers. In addition, even the weekday customers experience waiting times from one to ten minutes, although the probability of waiting a short time or a long time is smaller than waiting between about four and eight minutes.

My Ideas and Items to practice at the next team meeting

13. The next question is: " What does this mean to our customers? " By placing a vertical line on the histogram showing the customer requirement we will have a visual picture of how well our process is satisfying the customers:

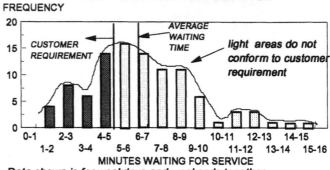

NOTES

Now we can actually see our process performance compared to the requirement of our customers. While the average waiting time is around six minutes, and that is only one minute longer than the customer requirement of five minutes, in fact that is not the correct comparison. The histogram above clearly shows that the majority of customers are not having their expectations met. The logical error in comparing the five minutes and the six minutes is that five minutes is a maximum that customers expect, while six minutes is the average that the process delivers.

Remember that a histogram is a 'snapshot in time'. The distribution will change as the process is improved. The objective for the above histogram is to move all of the vertical bars to the left of the vertical customer requirement line of five minutes. As the process is improved, the shape of this histogram will move to the left.

My Ideas and Items to practice at the next team meeting

HISTOGRAM OF DEGREES OF DEVIATION
FROM VERTICAL FOR FASTENERS ON
THE SIDES OF METAL CONTAINERS

Data collected by measuring 360 fastener angles.

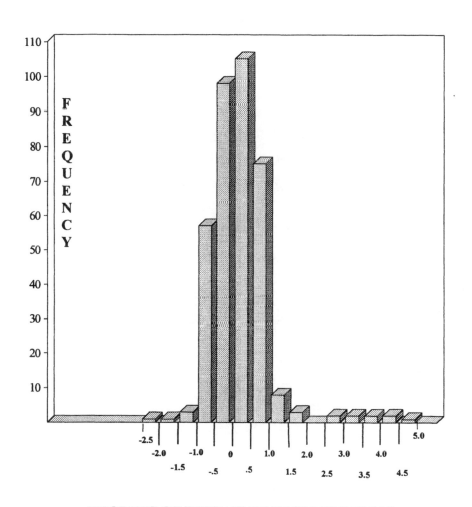

DEGREES OF DEVIATION FROM VERTICAL

My Ideas and Items to practice at the next team meeting

Data leads to information,
Information leads to knowledge,
Knowledge leads to understanding,
And understanding leads to wisdom.

Russell Ackoff
Systems Sciences Educator

12

SITUATION:

Team Members Say -

"What is our current status in each of these areas - and how can we display our current status in some graphic profile?"

"Also, a profile or pattern that conveys our Malcolm Baldrige scores with one compact graphic would be very useful."

"I'd like a way to show the performance at each major point in our work flow, in order to see bottlenecks, and to see changes over time."

SOLUTION:

Radar Chart

There is nothing permanent except change.
--Heraclitus

Radar Chart

What Is It:

A type of circular, or polar chart displaying the level of performance for each of several categories or areas. A unique pattern is formed for each set of categories and their scores. The patterns formed often look similar to patterns on radar screens, hence the name. Also called spider diagrams because of the spider web appearance of the patterns.

Why Use It:

- To display *current performance* prior to planning a change in a process or a system
- To *combine* with an evaluation of the degree of importance of items for success of a project. Such combining shows the current status of important items and strongly suggests which categories to address first in a project.
- To establish a snapshot of the current situation, with the goal of changing and improving that *pattern over time*

When:

- As a step before detailed planning of what to do and how to do it
- During data collection phases of process improvement or problem solving as one way to display the data
- During identification of problems or areas to address in a process
- When evaluating each macro step in a process to show the performance of each sequential step

Things do not change, we do.
--Henry David Thoreau

QUICK VIEW

RADAR CHART

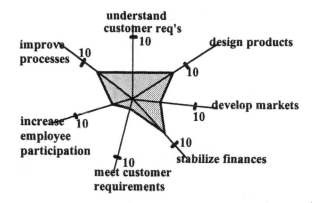

1. Place names of categories for evaluation along the outside perimeter of a circle.

2. From the center, draw a ray to each category.

3. Place a scale of 0-10 on each category.

4. Score each category in terms of current performance, where excellent and complete satisfaction is given a 10. Place a mark on each ray representing the score.

5. Connect the scores on each ray with a line. This will form a 'radar' pattern, which can be shaded.

6. The achieved performance is represented by the shaded pattern. The needed effort to be fully satisfactory and functional in all categories is represented by the blank area between the circle and this shaded pattern.

Achieve these Potentials

NOTES

....

....

....

....

....

....

POTENTIALS	ACHIEVING POTENTIALS
Involve other team members and stakeholders in understanding current status of the project	A Radar Chart provides a compact and highly informative picture of current status of categories or areas of a project. The categories are those that need to be addressed for a problem to be solved, or for a process to be improved, or for a project to be completed. They can be the activities from a Supportive Action Matrix (SAM). They may even be elements of a vision or of a strategic plan. The blank area outside of the inner 'radar area' represents the effort that is yet needed in each category before the project is complete. Team members and stakeholders can see the effort needed on this radar pattern. Also, they may be involved in collecting the data that generates the Radar Chart.
Show changes over time	A Radar Chart of performance <u>before</u> improvement efforts can be superimposed on one <u>after</u> improvements. Increases in size of the pattern represent the improvements, the efforts, and the energies that have occurred. If one area has been permitted to slide in order that efforts could be spent making large gains in other areas, the superimposed Radar Chart will reveal that situation.
Show different performance for different organizations in the company	Multiple Radar Charts can be superimposed to show different performances and to allow easy comparison. Usually, this superimposing is limited to three - beyond three, the chart is confusing. Multiple charts can, however, be placed all on separate sections of one page to allow easy comparison.
Performance of macro steps in a flow chart can be displayed in circular sequence	Imagine the sequential macro steps drawn in flow chart form for a process. For each macro step you can evaluate its performance, where '0' (zero) is completely unfunctional and '10' is excellent - such as high throughput or high accuracy. Each macro step name is placed around a circle; a ray (a straight line) drawn from the center to each name; the evaluation score placed on that ray as a point; and the points connected.

My Ideas and Items to practice at the next team meeting

....

....

POTENTIALS	ACHIEVING POTENTIALS
Performance of macro steps in a flow chart can be displayed in circular sequence	The pattern that results is tied to the sequencing of the steps in the flow chart. Unlike other types of Radar Charts where the categories can be placed in various sequences around the circle, in this case they are tied to the flow. The sequence is locked-in and can change only if macro steps are added or deleted in the flow. Such a Macro Flow Radar Chart can reveal bottlenecks in the flow of a process; troublesome steps that generate difficulties only to be handled by other steps down stream; high performing steps; and overall performance.

these Achieve Potentials

EXAMPLE OF APPLYING A RADAR CHART
TO THE MACRO-FLOW STEPS OF A PROCESS

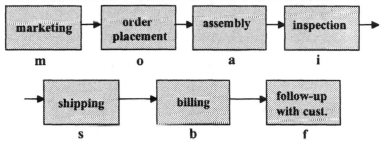

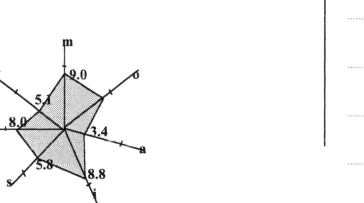

NOTES

My Ideas and Items to practice at the next team meeting

POTENTIALS	ACHIEVING POTENTIALS
The seven categories of the National Quality Award can be displayed with this chart	A company seeking to understand its current "TQM health" can do so by using the Malcolm Baldrige National Quality Award and conducting a self-evaluation across the many items within each category. Hundreds of companies have used the criteria of the MBNQA to evaluate their current quality status. One approach to displaying the scores and to show subsequent change over time, is with a Radar Chart.

Achieve these Potentials

NOTES

....

....

....

....

....

....

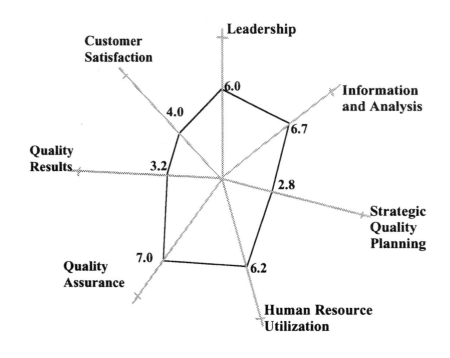

Excellence Areas Selected for Evaluation

My Ideas and Items to practice at the next team meeting

....

....

PITFALLS	AVOIDING PITFALLS
Disagreement on the evaluation for each category	If the categories are difficult to actually measure, and are the result of the team's knowledge base, the scoring may be wide spread. Elements of a vision, for example, may be: - Establish new programs - Recruit skilled workers - Improve physical plant - Improve training curriculum for all employees - Decrease unit costs - Streamline critical work processes - Support the community Evaluation of these elements can be difficult, but the effort can be extremely rewarding, as with self-assessment for the National Quality Award categories. For initial efforts, however, the team may need to use their current knowledge base in order to obtain areas for initial focus. If wide variation exists in this knowledge-based evaluation approach, collect more information. Evaluation can be eased by temporarily limiting the scope of the areas being evaluated. What 'programs' need to be evaluated the most. What part of the 'physical plant' is most critical.
Experimentation may lead to confusion	Experimentation with charts is a wonderful idea. Do it! Try new approaches and new ways! One guideline with a Radar Chart, however, is to always reserve the scale of '10' at the outside circle for 'perfection,' or high performance. By always equating '10' with excellence, the Radar Chart will be interpreted consistently and logically regardless of the categories that are used. We do not suggest that a Radar Chart be used in place of a Pareto Chart. A high Pareto category (like billing errors) would probably be assigned a high value on a Radar Chart - which is exactly opposite the intention of a Radar pattern.

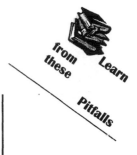

Learn from these Pitfalls

NOTES

....

....

....

....

....

....

....

....

My Ideas and Items to practice at the next team meeting

....

RADAR CHART

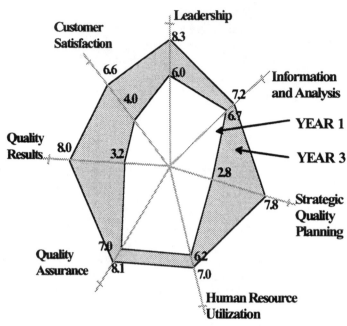

NOTES

·······································

·······································

·······································

·······································

·······································

·······································

HOW TO CONSTRUCT A RADAR CHART

1. Draw a circle.

2. Draw a ray from the center to the outside circle for each category to be evaluated.

3. Place the category names on the circle at the end of each ray.

4. Place "0" (zero) at the center and "10" (ten) at the end of each ray as it intersects the circle.

My Ideas and Items to practice at the next team meeting

···

···

5. Evaluate each category in terms of current performance. Ten is excellent. Zero is not functional. Consider using this scale:

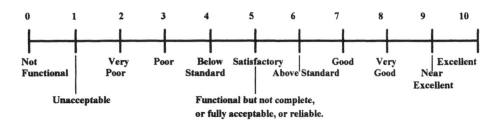

6. Place a point on each ray representing the evaluation score.

7. Simply connect the points, forming a multi-sided closed figure. Shade the figure on the inside of the 'radar area.'

8. Interpretation is as follows:

   - The shaded area shows current performance.
   - The blank area between the shaded area and the circle shows the effort to be done to achieve excellence in all categories.

NOTES

....

....

....

....

....

....

....

My Ideas and Items to practice at the next team meeting

....

Discovery consists of looking at the same thing as everyone else, and thinking something different.

Albert Szent-Gyorgyi
Nobel Prize for Medicine 1937

Thanks to <u>A Whack on the Side of the Head</u>, by Roger von Oech

13

SITUATION:

Team Members Say -

"Now we know a major problem with our process - in this case it is extreme time in updating our data base of client shipping addresses."

"Let's fix it."

"Right, but first we need to explore what is causing that problem. Then we will fix the cause."

"What tool can we use to explore causes?"

SOLUTION:

Cause and Effect Diagram

The problem is not whether business will survive in
competition with business, but whether any business
will survive at all in the face of social change.
--Laurence Joseph McGinley

Cause and Effect Diagram

What Is It:

A structured brainstorming approach that creates a diagram of possible causes of a specific problem.

Why Use It:

- To explore new *possibilities* and capabilities in a process
- To uncover the *primary causes* of a problem in the process
- To display the *weaknesses* and *opportunities* in a process
  - This display facilitates communication and ideas among team members about new possibilities for the process
  - The display also serves as a reference for next items to address after the primary cause is removed

When:

- Whenever ideas need to flow and the team needs to start some energy around exploring possibilities
- After a specific problem in the process has been selected - in order to find the Primary Cause
- In addition, the C/E Diagram is useful whenever a team issue or subproblem arises, such as: "What are the causes of the team having difficulty in this step?"

Change is an easy panacea. It takes character to stay in one place and be happy there.
--Elizabeth Clarke Dunn

CAUSE AND EFFECT DIAGRAM

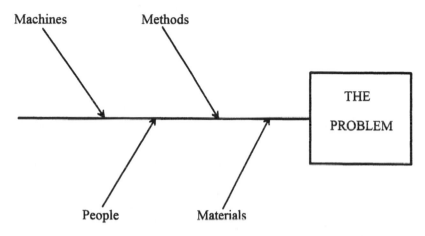

NOTES

....

....

1. Place the problem (the 'effect') in the box on the right side.

....

2. Select categories of causes. Generic ones are Machines (including computers), Methods (including policies), People, and Materials.

....

3. Identify plausible causes within each category.

....

4. Identify causes of causes. Try to get to 'root causes'.

....

5. When complete, circle three to five causes.

....

6. Collect data to verify those causes that are likely to be primary.

My Ideas and Items to practice at the next team meeting

....

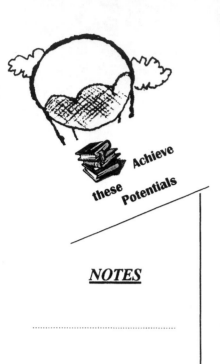

Achieve these Potentials

NOTES

....

....

....

....

....

....

POTENTIALS	ACHIEVING POTENTIALS
New possibilities are uncovered	The C/E Diagram invites expansive thinking about possible *causes* of a weakness or difficulty in the business process. Often causes are known, but *not* recognized as key items to correcting *customer dissatisfaction.* They are simply "things that happen and we take care of them later."
	By inviting others to join your team as you brainstorm possible but plausible causes, you form new horizons, new dialogs, and new internal customer relationships. Stakeholders, and those who work in the targeted problem area of the process are often excellent subject matter experts to invite to a construction of the C/E diagram. *Trust among peers increases.*
New approaches to using a C/E are uncovered	The C/E Diagram is very flexible. A team may choose the generic categories of Machines, Methods, People, and Materials, or they may choose others that they know would be more fitting. Sometimes a previous *Pareto Chart* with its categories of types of errors can provide the C/E categories. For example, there may be six different types of errors on a Pareto Chart that relate to "late delivery." Those six types could well be the categories on a *C/E diagram* that is addressing the causes of "late delivery."

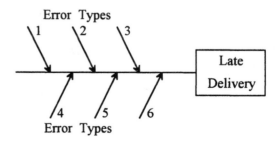

Also, the team may discover that one category is especially rich with difficulties. That category can be expanded into its own C/E Diagram.

My Ideas and Items to practice at the next team meeting

....

....

POTENTIALS	ACHIEVING POTENTIALS

Categories of Why Error Type 3 Occurs

A   B

C   D   E

Error Type 3, Missing Address

Primary, or Root Cause is uncovered

The whole objective of using a C/E Diagram is to find the primary cause of a problem. The primary cause, when removed, will significantly reduce the problem. It may not be the only cause, but it is significant.

To find the primary cause, first construct the C/E Diagram. Then three to five potential primary causes are circled by the team. The team may choose to invite others who are experienced with the particular problem they are addressing, to assist with the investigation.

In TQM, decisions are based on data. The next step is to *collect data* on the candidate primary causes to verify the significance of each. The objective is to isolate one Root Cause to address. The team can tackle other significant causes of the problem at a later date.

A large C/E Diagram with many possible causes

In itself, a large C/E Diagram is an opportunity to uncover new ideas. The difficulty, however, in focusing. First, have one large flip-chart sheet for each category. Brainstorm and explore causes of causes within one category at a time.

Second, after completing a category, discuss it before moving on to the next category. Decide which causes in that category are significant. Circle those. After completing all categories and circling candidate Root Causes, select 3-5 to explore via data collection.

these Achieve Potentials

NOTES

My Ideas and Items to practice at the next team meeting

Learn from these Pitfalls

NOTES

....

....

....

....

....

....

PITFALLS	AVOIDING PITFALLS
Many causes appear of equal importance to the team	If a few causes cannot be selected because *several* appear to be significant, there are approaches to use. First, invite others to review your C/E Diagram and to give their view. Second, causes can be related. Removing one can reduce another automatically. Identify those linkages. Several causes that will be reduced by reducing one is a chain effect that can help the team select where to begin. Third, collect preliminary data on the causes to determine which ones actually occur more frequently and have greater impact.
Primary cause too rapidly identified as 'No time' or 'No Money'	While lack of time or of resources may be a true primary cause, they may also *not* be the primary cause for the problem at hand. Sometimes we quickly believe the cause is lack of time, but *lack of priority* is the real issue. And priorities will not be reset unless the *cost* of ignoring the problem is clear. So the real cause of the process problem may be lack of data to show others so they can reset priorities. *If 'time' or 'money' are identified as primary causes by the team, explore underlying causes and issues .*
Extensive discussions around the items being placed on the C/E Diagram. It is taking a long time to construct. People are frustrated	Remember the rules of basic Brainstorming: no criticism, no idea is a bad idea, everyone has a turn, passing (giving no idea when it is your turn) is acceptable, and build on each others ideas. Practice those 'rules' when constructing the C/E Diagram. Also, remind the team to *stay focused* on what they are doing. The purpose as they construct the C/E Diagram is not to question each other, but to document all the ideas by constructing the C/E Diagram. It <u>is</u> appropriate for team members to ask clarifying questions during this Brainstorming, but not to become side-tracked.

My Ideas and Items to practice at the next team meeting

.. ..

... .

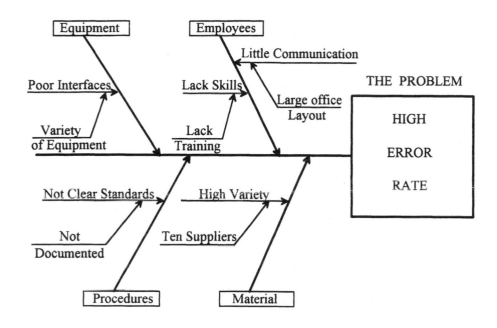

THE PROBLEM

HIGH

ERROR

RATE

HOW TO CONSTRUCT A CAUSE AND EFFECT DIAGRAM

1. State the problem (the 'effect') clearly. The team may have to take some time to discuss the problem and to write a problem statement in order for the problem to be clear to all team members. The Cause and Effect (C/E) Diagram is a particular way of using brainstorming, and as is true in any brainstorming, the problem or issue being addressed must be as clear as possible with the team.

2. Draw the form of the C/E Diagram.

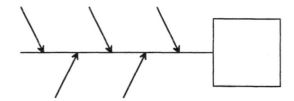

My Ideas and Items to practice at the next team meeting

3. Determine the categories for the main lines of the diagram. These categories may be the generic ones of Machine, Materials, Methods, and People. Other categories may be selected based on knowledge of the team, or data that has been collected. Sometimes the categories of errors from a Pareto Chart are useful as the categories on a C/E Diagram.

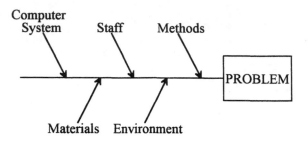

NOTES

....

....

....

....

....

....

4. Brainstorm the causes of the problem. Experience has shown that it is effective to brainstorm causes in one category - such as 'Methods' - completely before moving on to another category. This will be 'informed' brainstorming, that is, actual experience of the team will steer the recorded ideas. That is the purpose of a C/E Diagram.

 After capturing the main causes within a category, ask why each cause occurs. The idea is to get to primary or root causes by asking 'why' several times. Asking 'why' gets to deeper levels.

5. Circle those items on the diagram that are believed to be the primary causes. Two or three items may be circled.

6. Collect data on the selected items to verify that they occur with sufficient frequency or strength to cause a significant portion of the problem.

My Ideas and Items to practice at the next team meeting

....

....

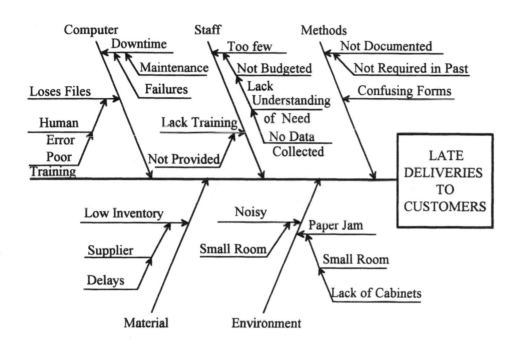

Computer   Staff   Methods

Downtime   Too few   Not Documented

Maintenance   Not Budgeted   Not Required in Past

Failures   Lack   Confusing Forms

Loses Files   Understanding

Human   of Need

Error   Lack Training

Poor   No Data

Training   Not Provided   Collected

LATE
DELIVERIES
TO
CUSTOMERS

Low Inventory   Noisy

Supplier   Small Room   Paper Jam

Delays   Small Room

Lack of Cabinets

Material   Environment

NOTES

....

....

....

....

....

....

....

My Ideas and Items to practice at the next team meeting

....

Since decision making is done at all levels, the information system must feed all of these levels.

Joseph M. Juran
TQM expert and advocate

14

SITUATION:

Team Members Say -

"We need to decide which problem to approach first - we cannot work on five at one time.**"**

"How do we decide?**"**

"We need criteria.**"**

"We also need a way to see our decision, a way to make our deciding factors visible for all of us.**"**

SOLUTION:

Decision Matrix

What we hope ever to do with ease, we must learn first to do with diligence.
--Samuel Johnson

Decision Matrix

What Is It:

A matrix or table, that allows a team to understand the issues and the facts involved in selecting one item to pursue from among several items.

Why Use It:

- It is a *comprehensive* approach that facilitates a decision by the team
- It is an important step in reaching *consensus*
- To utilize *data* in order to facilitate *decisions*
- To provide a graphical and *visible layout* of the issues and facts

When:

- Anytime a decision is to be made by a team and there are multiple criteria to apply to multiple options
- During selection of a particular problem
- During selection of a particular change to a process

A person to carry on a successful business must have imagination. They must see things as in a vision, a dream of the whole thing.
--Charles M. Schwab

<u>*QUICK VIEW*</u>

DECISION MATRIX

Issue or Solution	Criteria 1	Criteria 2	Criteria 3	Criteria 4	Rank
A					
B					
C					

<u>*NOTES*</u>

1. Select criteria.

2. Place data in the cells of the matrix.

3. Place ranking in each cell.

    1 = undesirable

    5 = desirable

4. Consider weighting each criteria.

5. Total the cell values across to the right.

6. Check for team consensus.

My Ideas and Items to practice at the next team meeting

....

POTENTIALS	ACHIEVING POTENTIALS
Data points are available for use in the Matrix	The cells of the Decision Matrix are intended for data, whenever it is available. Cost estimates, for example, are simply estimates. Be certain they are reasonably accurate, but use whatever data is available. Detailed cost accounting, or any detailed analysis is often not needed. Remember that 'cost' can be either cost to fix an ongoing problem or cost *not* to fix it. The latter is referred to as the cost of non-conformance. If the problem causing that non-conformance is removed, then a savings results. Two separate criteria, therefore, can be "cost to fix" and "savings if fixed". The net of these two is an important financial criteria. If strictly measurable information - like dollars, number of items, etc. - is not available, then use a ranking scale. For example, the customer may have great interest in having a particular problem fixed, and little interest in another. Talk to the customer, if possible. Can a dollar value be attached to each? If not, can they - or can you, based on interviews with the customer - place each on a scale. The 1 to 5 scale shown under Quick View, and discussed later, is often sufficient.
Consensus is reached	The Matrix makes the data and relative rankings visible. The entire picture becomes one. A condensed view of the options and their effects is present for each team member. Further, the team has this *visualization of choices* to show to anyone interested. Team decisions become easier to explain to others. It is important to remember that while the Decision Matrix gives a total value for each item, and that one might have the highest total score, only team agreement counts in the end. In other words, the *team members need not accept the highest scoring item as the one to select first*. There may be some new insights to discover through the conversation. Is the data correct? Are the weightings of the criteria (see Quick View previously, and construction, later) correct? Is a criterion missing?

Achieve these Potentials

NOTES

....

....

....

....

....

....

....

My Ideas and Items to practice at the next team meeting

....

....

POTENTIALS	ACHIEVING POTENTIALS
Teamwork results from the gathering and use of information needed in the matrix	Interviews with customers, suppliers, subprocess workers, inspectors, quality assurance data analysts, and perhaps with benchmarking companies all take time. The benefit or gain is this: While we have often in the past made decisions without data, TQM supports a change. TQM and Process Improvement call for *decisions based on data.* This Matrix embodies and facilitates that philosophy. Teamwork results from the gathering of the data, the use of it in making decisions, and the belief on the part of the team in their results and recommendations. To begin this teamwork, the team members need to agree on the criteria being used in the matrix. They also need to plan the data gathering.
Differences in rankings by team members may lead to discovery of new ideas and areas	After data is collected and entered into the cells of the Matrix, ranking (1 to 5) is applied to each cell. Even though data is present, interpretation of the data may differ among team members. Rankings may differ. Conflict may arise. *Managing that conflict is important.* View the differences not as destructive but as *constructive* - which it is. Team members have different interpretations of data for a reason. What is it? *Listen to each other.* Write the key points from each viewpoint on an easel. Look at those points. Do not look for compromise too soon. Look for new ideas. Expect the unexpected.

these Achieve Potentials

NOTES

....

....

....

....

....

....

....

My Ideas and Items to practice at the next team meeting

....

PITFALLS	AVOIDING PITFALLS
Confusion on ranking a cost criteria as 'high' or 'low'	High cost is not desirable. Some team members may score it as 'high' in the cell of a Decision Matrix. Others will score it low.
	Then there is, for example, a high dollar amount of savings. Is that scored 'high' or 'low'?
	To avoid this confusion, use the scale of 1 to 5 where 1 is undesirable, and 5 is desirable.
	With this approach, a high cost expenditure is scored as 1, while a high savings is 5.
	Remember, in a Decision Matrix you are evaluating the desirability of expected results.
Averaging different ranking by team members circumvents understanding	The Decision Matrix offers value not only by being a visual representation of the team's decision process, but also by facilitating discussion among team members around differences of opinion. Value different scores of different team members. Ask why. *Explore each other's ideas.*
	A criteria that summarizes 'cost to fix' and 'savings if fixed' is useful, but the ratio of the two can be misleading. For example, which of the two cases below would you prefer:

	Cost	Savings
A	$1	$100
B	$10	$1000

Both A and B have a cost/savings ratio of 1/100, which is quite attractive. But B nets $990 while A nets only $99.

In short, use a summary column of net savings, not of a ratio.

My Ideas and Items to practice at the next team meeting

....

....

NOTES

....

....

....

....

....

....

	NET SAVINGS	IMPACT ON CUST.	DIFFIC- ULTY	COMPET- ITIVE EDGE	TOTAL
WEIGHT	4	10	4	9	
DEVELOP NEW TRAIN'G	$ 20 K 3 12	5 50	$ 40 K 4 16	4 36	114
CHANGE COMPUT- ERS	$ 0 1 4	4 40	$ 100 K 2 8	3 27	79
CHANGE SOFT- WARE	$ 10K 2 8	5 50	$ 50 K 3 12	4 36	106

HOW TO CONSTRUCT A DECISION MATRIX

The team (usually a Process Improvement Team) has a list of items and needs to select one. It may be a list of problems within the process, a list of potential solutions, a list of processes that are being considered for improvement, or geographic locations that could trial a solution, and the like. These items are placed down the left side. The objective is to use a Decision Matrix to select one of the items from the list.

1. The team generates and selects a set of criteria to use. Brainstorming, plus combining ideas and voting, is usually an effective way to generate the set of criteria.

   ☑ *Tip: The set of criteria generally should not exceed about eight items or the matrix becomes cumbersome.*

   ☑ *Tip: Criteria that are useful are: impact on the customer, cost to fix, cost to not fix, net savings, feasibility, resources required, time required, and competitive advantage that can be formed.*

My Ideas and Items to practice at the next team meeting

2. Next, the team collects data and information on each of the criteria for each of the items on the left side. The cells of the matrix are filled in with data. Customer impact, as an example, may be difficult to quantify, but quantifying is the intention here. If possible, obtain a monetary value from the customer on the value of attacking a problem, or of implementing a solution, and do it for each item.

> ☑   *Tip: When preferences are the issue rather than hard data, use the 1 to 5 scale described below. Use it directly in those cells where data is absent.*

3. Based on the data, rank each item against each criteria. A scale of 1 to 5 is suggested where '1' means the cost or value is 'very undesirable' and '5' means it is 'very desirable.' This approach avoids difficulties with 'low cost' being, for example, a 'high' on a scale of 'High, Medium, Low' (H,M,L).

4. The team should always consider weighting the criteria. 'Customer Impact' or 'Competitive Edge' may be more important than 'Cost Savings,' for example. The team needs to discuss the weighting. For example, the most important may be a '10' and the least important a '1.' Two criteria can certainly be weighted equally.

We have found that weighting of criteria is not difficult for teams, but several points are important. First, remember to base the weights on data and information, just as all decisions in TQM are based on data. Talk to customers, the process owner (see Appendix and Chapter 2), and those working in the process. Use the Customer Requirements Matrix (Chapter 5). The last column of that matrix provides guidance on the importance (the 'weight') of each requirement from the customer's point of view. Second, remember to honor differences that arise in team members weighting of criteria. If one person gives a high weight to an item, and another gives a relatively low weight, then there is something to be learned. Discuss the difference and use data and information to help understand each other and to help resolve the different view point. Almost always, the difference is caused by some slight difference in the meaning of a phrase, or a word, but the difference may be due to different understanding of the data. Also see the Chapter on Prioritization Matrices in the "Memory Jogger Plus" by GOAL/QPC for a step-by-step approach to assigning weightings. In this approach, each person compares each criteria to every other and assigns a relative weight. All of the pair-by-pair ratings from all people are then combined.

5. Multiply the cell rankings by the criteria weighting and add scores to the right.

6. Check for team consensus. Numbers are not the answer; the common understanding that is formed during the process is what matters.

My Ideas and Items to practice at the next team meeting

....

....

NOTES

DECISION MATRIX PRACTICE EXERCISE

Note: A Decision Matrix can be used early in a team's overall problem solving activities for clarifying a variety of decisions. It can also be the point at which much of the team's previous work and findings are coming together. To help provide a means for a team to practice this tool, we have chosen to include an exercise here. It is based on a real situation.

PROCESS FOR RESOLVING BILLING COMPLAINTS

Input: Data base information about customer accounts.

Output: Information (resolutions) to external customers.

Background: This national insurance company has ten complaint resolution centers around the country. Each center receives about 5000 calls a month. The centers have normal business hours.

A Process Improvement Team representing the Northeast Center is identifying problems in methods, capacity, data base content, and equipment. These areas are explained further below.

Note: The objective is to complete a Decision Matrix that allows consensus on selection of one of the problems below.

If more data is needed than is presented here, you are invited to improvise. Construct the data yourself. Consider cost-to-fix, savings-if-fixed, feasibility, resources required, etc.

THE PROBLEMS:

Methods

Improper use of data bases such as using wrong data fields, reading wrong accounts, or interpreting code improperly - results in an estimated average of 25 incorrect statements given verbally to customers at the Northeast Center each month. The methods and training used are identical in all centers. The incorrect verbal statements have led to further complications, including callbacks, complaints to the CEO and letters to consumer groups. Several court cases have resulted involving both large and small accounts.

NOTES

My Ideas and Items to practice at the next team meeting

Capacity

The system is overloaded during three daily peak hours. Callers wait in queue during those peaks, and abandoned calls run 70 percent. Callers complain to upper management.

Data Bases

The customer profile data at any instant has a 0.1% error level causing mistakes in customer addresses, in identification numbers, and in insurance payments due. The 0.1% error causes confusion during some calls and causes incorrect information to customers. Complaints go to upper management.

Equipment

The keyboards and terminals of the complaint/resolution assistants are deteriorating. Calls are lost. Screens occasionally go blank. The system "goes down" an average of one quarter hour each week, usually 2-3 minutes at a time. The result is complaints, callbacks, employee frustration, and extra effort.

Issue	Cost to Fix	Savings when Fixed	Net Savings	Importance to Customer	Ease of Implementing	TOTAL
WT.						
Methods						
Capacity						
Data Base						
Equipment						

Note: The criteria above are examples. What would you use? What weighting would you apply to each criteria?

My Ideas and Items to practice at the next team meeting

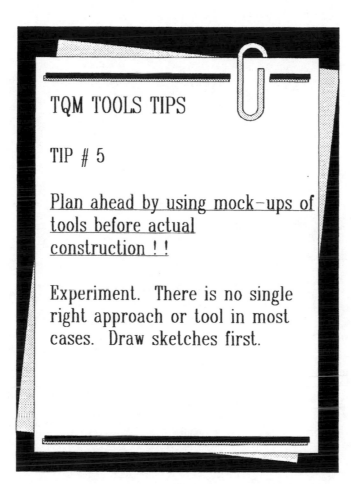

TQM TOOLS TIPS

TIP # 5

<u>Plan ahead by using mock-ups of tools before actual construction ! !</u>

Experiment. There is no single right approach or tool in most cases. Draw sketches first.

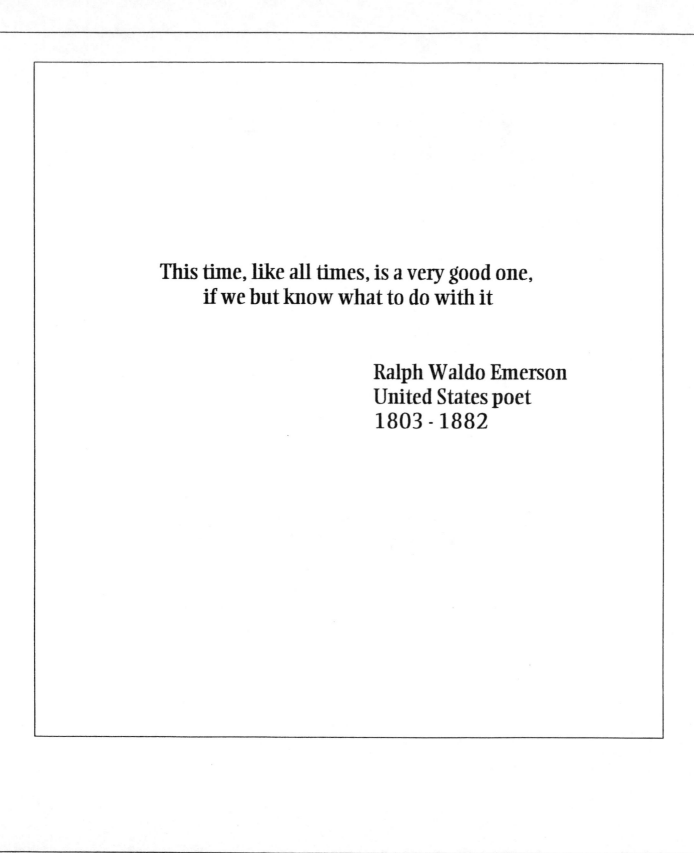

This time, like all times, is a very good one,
if we but know what to do with it

Ralph Waldo Emerson
United States poet
1803 - 1882

15

Situation:

Team Members Say -

"We need a way to capture the tasks we want accomplished and how they will be achieved."

"We can make a list."

"We need more than a list. How can we have a really effective way to both plan and track our tasks."

Solution:

Supportive Action Matrix (SAM)

Business is like riding a bicycle--either you keep
moving or you fall down.
--Anonymous

Supportive Action Matrix (SAM)

What Is It:

A layout of the tasks necessary to achieve a goal, along with the assigned people, the schedule, pertinent information, and identification of support structures.

Why Use It:

- To *record tasks* necessary to accomplish a goal or project
- To create clear *communication:*
    - In teams
    - In organizations
    - With process stakeholders
- To *document the support* mechanisms people may need to achieve the tasks
- To show *linkage* of tasks:
    - Sequencing
    - Interdependencies

When:

- Useful at each team meeting, and at each step of PDCA
- Especially useful for implementing an action plan, such as:
    - Customer needs analysis
    - Data collection
    - Trial of a solution
    - Implementing a solution
- When an overall objective will be a accomplished through completion of several tasks, and linkage and support must be clear

Those who write clearly have readers, those who write obscurely have commentators.
--Albert Camus

SUPPORTIVE ACTION MATRIX

Team Name _____   Page _____ of _____

Team Leader _____

Task No.	Task Description	Assigned To	Support From	Date Assigned	Planned Completion Date	Measure of Success	Review Date	Comments (Projected outcome; Dependencies; Revised date; Lessons learned)

NOTES

....

....

....

....

....

....

....

My Ideas and Items to practice at the next team meeting

....

NOTES

....

....

....

....

....

....

POTENTIALS	ACHIEVING POTENTIALS
The Matrix is actively used and supported by team members	The Supportive Action Matrix (SAM) represents the culmination of planning for a project. Use of it greatly facilitates the success of a plan. For a team to support and use the SAM, it must view it as a valuable tool. The key question is, what makes this tool valuable? Teams are accustomed to Action Plans, which are often viewed as assigning responsibility for task and documentation of unrealistic due dates.

The SAM is different. The Matrix records tasks and due dates, but it also documents the support required by the person assigned the task. The keys to successful use of the SAM, and therefore overall project success, are:

a) Consensus for all entries
b) Agreement by support areas for their role
c) One person who 'owns' the SAM process of recording, reaching consensus, and tracking the tasks. This owner is usually the team leader.
d) Encouragement to learn from failures, and use of the SAM to record schedules missed, etc., and the lessons learned.

Use of the Matrix for Deployment Planning	Managers and teams rarely plan *deployment* well. 'Development planning', however, is usually well done. We know this from data and interviews taken across a variety of companies and planning groups. Development planning addresses <u>what</u> to do. It is about generating new ideas, new products, new services and establishing a <u>goal</u>.

'Deployment planning', however, is rarely comprehensive. This phrase addresses <u>how</u> to accomplish the goal. It is about planning the implementation (or deployment) steps, and seeing the relationship, timing, and interaction of those steps.

The Supportive Action Matrix is a tool for displaying and facilitating <u>how</u> to achieve a goal. When completed for an overall project, all tasks and steps are shown, *linkages are seen* and supportive infrastructure is established.

My Ideas and Items to practice at the next team meeting

....

....

POTENTIALS	ACHIEVING POTENTIALS
Use of the Matrix for Implementation	After deployment planning is complete, actual implementation can begin. The SAM provides a mechanism for tracking progress. It also greatly facilitates understanding of modifications needed during implementation and documentation of *lessons learned* along the way.
Use of the Matrix for Action Items that arise during team meetings	The SAM is useful, not only for planning an overall project as discussed above, but also to capture and facilitate execution of needed actions, or tasks, that arise during team meetings. For example, certain data may be needed in two weeks. Place that action on the SAM along with the names of those who will gather the information, and any support they need to perform the task. Each action item is reviewed at the start of each meeting. *Remember, the reviews are always supportive in nature. Ask how you can help.*

NOTES

Note how well the SAM supports the Shewhart cycle of Plan-Do-Check-Act. During the Planning phase, the SAM captures and shows relationships among the deployment steps. During the 'Doing' or implementation phase, the SAM tracks progress and provides visible ways to track whether barriers are occurring. During the 'checking' or evaluation phase, the SAM is used to both show progress and to show steps that needed to be taken for other data collection. Finally, during the 'Act' or modification phase, the SAM provides an overall documentation of why the modifications were needed and helps in retaining lessons learned.

My Ideas and Items to practice at the next team meeting

PITFALLS	AVOIDING PITFALLS
Can be mechanical, not true consensus	Use this tool to raise issues in the team. If someone has difficulty supporting a due date, work to uncover that concern and to open a discussion. Manage any conflict that arises by always working to learn from different viewpoints.
Unrealistic due dates	This is the most familiar pitfall. *Explore why the dates are not realistic.* Perhaps those assigned the task need support from their supervision. Or perhaps they need data earlier. Weigh the importance of meeting a particular due date against the effort, cost, and time conflict with other tasks. Which task should be started first? Consider obtaining assistance from outside your team.
Tasks may be sequenced and one may create a bottleneck for the others	A common pattern in an overall project is one task depending on another. The SAM captures those dependencies. By identifying a critical (potential bottleneck) task, the team can place extra effort in completing that task, thereby preventing a slowdown of the overall project completion date.

Learn from these Pitfalls

NOTES

....

....

....

....

....

....

My Ideas and Items to practice at the next team meeting

....

....

Task No.	Task Description	Assigned To	Support From	Date Assigned	Planned Completion Date	Measure of Success	Review Date	Comments (Projected outcome; Dependencies; Revised date; Lessons learned)
5	Conduct measurement of inputs A, and B, from our east coast suppliers to see if our requirements are being met.	Roger	Kathy Bill M. Loret	Jan. 6	March 3	-Measures on inputs that relate to process needs. -200 data points across five weeks.	Jan. 20	Measurements to be taken have been selected and approved by all team members. Bill will arrange collection on the weekends.
							Feb.15	Collection for all 'A' inputs is complete. 'B' is underway. Suppliers have been contacted.

HOW TO CONSTRUCT A SUPPORTIVE ACTION MATRIX

<u>For an Overall Project</u>
The detailed tasks needed to achieve the project must first be identified. These tasks can be displayed on a Tree Diagram. For example:

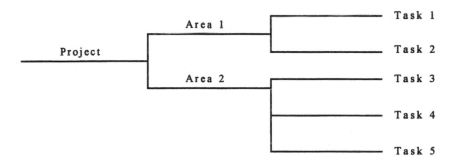

Each task is then entered in the Supportive Action Matrix (SAM). The columns are described below. Completing the SAM facilitates effective deployment planning.

My Ideas and Items to practice at the next team meeting

....

NOTES

....

....

....

....

....

....

For Team Meetings

During each meeting, someone (scribe, a team member, team leader) records action items as they arise. Toward the conclusion of the meeting these action items are reviewed both for completeness and for clarity. The final record of the actions is placed in the SAM before the meeting adjourns. The matrix is reviewed during the beginning of each team meeting. Status is discussed briefly and recorded in the "comments" column of the SAM. The column marked "review date" is intended for the review of the owner (primary responsibility) of the task. Do not lose sight, however, of who is providing support to the task owner. See the "support from" column. It may even be the whole team.

Description of the Columns

Task No.   - Any indexing or numbering scheme you choose. If two projects exist, A and B, the tasks could be numbered as A1, A2,...B1, B2.

Task   - <u>What</u> will be done?
Description   <u>How</u> will it be achieved, basically?

Assigned to   - The task owner. The person with primary responsibility to achieve the task.

Support from   - The person, or persons, supporting the task owner. This may be their manager, or someone from another area that has authority to make changes around the task at hand.

Planned Com-   - "Planned Completion Date." The original date for planned completion Date   pletion of the task.

Measure of   - This is the goal or target for the task, but it is in a measurable
Success   format. Examples are: 25% reduction in cost; All data sets loaded and checked; All contacts made; All surveys collected and computer entered; 200 employees surveyed; etc. You may have more than one measure of success for any one project.

Review Date   - The date of the last supportive review. This review is conducted with the Support person.

Comments   - This area of the SAM is updated during each review - both status reviews with the team and supportive reviews - as needed.

My Ideas and Items to practice at the next team meeting

....

....

An error does not become a mistake until you refuse to correct it.

Orlando Battista
Pharmaceutical researcher
and author

There are other beaches to explore. There are more shells to find.
This is only the beginning.

Anne Morrow Lindberg
from her book, <u>Gift from the Sea</u>

GLOSSARY

Affinity Diagram

A collection of note cards into vertical groupings. Header cards at the top of each vertical column describe the theme of each grouping. This tool is extremely useful for gathering and organizing a large number of ideas and comments related to achieving a project or vision.

Baldrige Quality Award Score

One measurement of the effectiveness of a quality system is the point score that an organization receives from an assessment against the Malcolm Baldrige National Quality Award criteria. The purpose of the Baldrige Quality Award is to promote quality awareness to recognize quality achievements of United States companies, and to publicize successful quality strategies. In order to receive the award, the quality system of a company, or of a major business unit within a company, must meet high standards in about thirty different areas. An organization's score on the application for the Baldrige Quality Award is one measurement of the company's progress toward world-class quality.

bar chart

Bar charts - showing either vertical or horizontal bars - are simple and effective ways to display a variety of data types.

basic flow chart

A flow of activities and decisions showing more detail than a Column Flow Chart. The flow begins with some input - like data, or material - and ends with an output - a finished product or service to the customer. Decisions are shown with diamond-shaped figures. Also called an Intermediate-Level Flow Chart because the level of detail is more than a Column Flow Chart but less than a micro flow chart that shows every movement of people and of equipment.

benchmarking

The term 'benchmarking' means to compare one or more of your processes against some other organization's method of doing essentially the same tasks in order to gain insights on how to improve. You can also use benchmarking to measure your organization's current way of doing business to establish a baseline of its performance. You can use this benchmark to determine both positive and negative variations in the organization's performance over time.

You can analyze 'world-class' operations in both competitors' and non-competitors' businesses to identify areas in which these businesses lead in a given industry. From this data, you can identify specific areas to improve and set performance goals.

cause and effect diagram

A structured brainstorming approach that creates a diagram of possible causes of a specific problem.

column flow chart

A high level or macro flow chart of a process in which the activities are placed in columns that represent the organizations, or the functions involved.

continuous improvement

The idea that quality management and improvement is necessarily a continuous activity to ensure ongoing customer satisfaction and improved efficiency. The Shewhart cycle of Plan, Do, Check, and Act described in the Preface is the basis for all continuous improvement activities.

control

The state of stability, normal variation, predictability and consistency. The process of regulating and guiding operations and processes using quantitative data and control mechanisms to detect and avoid potential adverse effects of change.

cost of quality

Cost of Quality is the actual dollars spent to satisfy customers. There are three components: Planning costs, Inspection costs, and cost to correct Failures.

critical business process

A process designated by management as critical to customer satisfaction, competitive effectiveness, or the achievement of strategic goals. Critical business processes are often cross-functional, spanning major functional organizations such as marketing, design, manufacturing, and distributing.

customer, external

A purchaser of your product or service

customer, internal

A downstream internal operation or person that depends on output or results of a given process.

customer needs

Customer needs are the essential characteristics of a product or service that must be present in order for the product or service to be fully useful to the customer. Customers may describe their needs and expectations in language ranging from general qualitative concepts to specific quantitative requirements. We use the Customer Requirements Matrix to assist in the translation of 'needs' to 'measurable needs'. See 'Customer Requirements'.

customer-process-supplier model

A representation of tasks and work flows. It shows a process, its customers, and its supplies, linked through process inputs and outputs, and through information flows in the form of requirements and feedback.

customer requirements

Customer needs that are stated in a measurable way. For example, 'timely' may be a need, but as a Process Improvement Team we must understand how to measure 'timely'. One answer for a given customer may be 'in less than five days'.

customer requirements matrix

A matrix, or table, for capturing customer needs in specific terms. It can be used with internal or external customers.

customer satisfaction measurement

You can ask both internal and external customers to indicate their level of pleasure or displeasure with your organization's products or services. Managers can use this data to determine how well the organization's processes are generating products and services that satisfy customers.

decision matrix

A matrix or table that allows a team to understand the issues and the facts involved in selecting one item to pursue from among several items.

Deming Prize

Prestigious annual quality award administered by the Japanese Union of Scientists and Engineers and named in honor of the late American statistician W. Edwards Deming. International awards for this prize are made although it is mainly a Japanese national award.

Dynamic Process Improvement Method

This is a six step method for improving processes that captures the essential steps that any method must have. It is, therefore, a universal or generalized approach.

employee satisfaction

Products and services must meet customer expectations. However, the personal relationships between employees and customers can make the difference in customer loyalty to a company. Therefore, employee satisfaction is critical to achieving and sustaining customer satisfaction. Key employee satisfiers include peer respect and recognition, opportunities to develop required skills and knowledge, support for projects and team activities from management, and challenging work assignments.

empowerment

Empowerment means giving employees the authority within the scope of their work functions to implement whatever is needed (legally and ethically) to meet customer expectations. Empowered employees decide and act with authority. Managers empower their employees in order for the organization to appropriately respond to the rapidly changing demands of customers and the competitive market. Managers also define how they will empower employees who participate in cross-functional teams.

feedback

Information from customers about how process output meets their needs.

histogram

A graphical display showing how frequently your data points fall into specified measurement intervals. It shows the distribution of the data, that is, what measurement occurs most often, least often, etc.

line chart

A line - it can be straight or wavy - showing the change, usually over time, of a variable that is being measured within the process. When the change is shown over time, such as hours or days, the name 'run' or 'trend' chart applies. 'Line chart' is the general name that applies.

Pareto diagram

A bar chart in descending order, showing the frequency of occurrence for each of several events, to allow relative comparison.

pie chart

A pictorial display of the proportional occurrence of events or conditions.

process

A set of interconnected activities with an input and an output. A process is best seen with a flow chart.

process capability

The measurement of process capability enables a process manager to evaluate whether the process can meet customer needs and requirements. Basically, the measurement shows whether the process output falls within Customer Requirements.

Process Improvement Team (PIT)

A Process Improvement Team is a group of employees who meet to identify problems in a process and to change that process for the better. PITs may establish themselves with the support of their management. Often, senior managers or the Quality Council establish PITs. Other names for PITs are perfectly acceptable, such as Process Action Team (PAT) used in Government Services, or Employee Process Improvement Team

(EPIT) used in several financial corporations, or Quality Improvement Team (QIT) used at AT&T and certain other companies.

process owner

The person with authority to change the process under recommendation of the team. The Process Owner provides leadership, support, and direction to the Process Improvement Team and with the Team Leader, often functions as a liaison with other teams and with the Quality Council.

project management

Project management is usually viewed as the planning, organizing, directing and controlling of company resources for a relatively short term objective (a project). Project management focuses on a single, time-bound set of activities related to one specific product, service, or management activity. Alternatively, Process Improvement focuses on the management of an organization's functions and processes to specifically assure efficient generation of products and services that satisfy customers. While Process Improvement may be a short term project, the intention is for continuous improvement.

quality

Quality means the degree of customer satisfaction. It is the degree of excellence of a product or service, characterized by reliability, durability, and freedom from defects. Also see Total Quality Management (TQM).

Quality Council

A Quality Council, which is usually made up of the organization's senior managers, leads and coordinates quality initiatives. The Quality Council, also known as a Total Quality Steering Team, meets regularly, ensures constant improvement of processes, arranges training, follow up, communications, direction, and support for TQM efforts.

Quality Manager

A Quality Manager, or Senior Quality Consultant, is a catalyst for quality improvement in the organization. Whether part-time or full-time, they help provide training, facilitating, consulting with managers and teams, and support for the Quality Council in its leadership efforts.

radar chart
>A type of circular, or polar chart displaying the degree of satisfactory performance for each of several categories or areas. A unique pattern is formed for each set of categories and their scores. The patterns formed often look similar to patterns on radar screens, hence the name. Also called spider diagrams because of the spider web appearance of the patterns.

reengineering
>Reengineering or process redesign is the method used to systematically overhaul or revamp an entire process, organization, or function. Essentially, it is aggressive Process Improvement.

reward and recognition
>Rewards and recognition are two ways to formally reinforce the values of the organization and to encourage customer-focused behavior. In an environment that promotes quality improvement, managers reward and recognize employees who focus on the customer, participate effectively on teams, prevent errors, and communicate.

service
>A deliverable sold or provided to customers that is usually intangible or transitory, as opposed to a product. This includes the services customers actively buy and the support services (for example, sales, delivery, and repair) that customers expect in the course of doing business.

Shewhart cycle
>Named after Walter Shewhart, who is discussed in the Preface of this book. The Shewhart cycle is the basis of all quality efforts. The cycle, shown in pictorial form in the Preface, is: Plan, Do, Check, Act.

supplier
>The source of material and/or information to a process. A supplier may be internal or external to the company, organization, or group.

Supportive Action Matrix (SAM)

> A layout of the tasks necessary to achieve a goal, along with the assigned people, the schedule, pertinent information, and identification of support structures for those assigned the task.

team

> TEAM: Together Everyone Accomplishes More.

teamwork

> Teamwork means working together to achieve a common goal. Teamwork applies within teams and on the job. In terms of the job, teamwork means working together in the most effective way to deliver what is important to customers.

Total Quality Management (TQM)

> The whole system of increasing customer satisfaction, employee involvement and satisfaction, process improvement, and strategic quality direction.

vision

> The desired future state of the business.

The Author

William L. Montgomery received his Masters and his Doctorate in engineering and biomedical engineering from the University of Pittsburgh after his Bachelors degree from Lehigh University. He also attained a Masters Degree in Management Sciences from Pace University in New York City. He joined Bell Labs in 1968 where he earned various patents before joining AT&T where, in 1984 he joined the Corporate headquarters structure and served as an internal consultant and trainer. Before retiring from AT&T, Bill influenced the quality efforts and trained the facilitators of most of the business units in the company. Starting his own company in 1990, he has trained and consulted with about ten thousand people in 200 companies. He and his wife Loretta have four daughters who are on their own with a variety of interests and occupations.

The Montgomery Group

The Montgomery Group fully supports the ideals and philosophy of the National Graduate School of Quality Management. The Group is a network of specialist consultants and trainers known for effective approaches that improve organizations. The approaches involve tools, techniques, evaluations, training, and coaching. The emphasis is on enlightening and exciting customers, employees, and managers while improving processes, market position, and profits. Specific areas handled by the trainers and consultants include Effective Strategic Planning, Process Improvement, Team Building, Management Skills training, Facilitator training, and Team Leader training. The company is centered in Doylestown, Pennsylvania and has served organizations throughout the United States and Internationally. For more information, call 215-489-0826.

The National Graduate School

The National Graduate School of Quality Management has been recognized as the nation's only graduate school devoted to the Master of Science in Quality Systems Management. The Congressional Record states " The National Graduate School is unique in requiring tangible, team-driven results from all ... candidates prior to graduation. It is a higher-education benchmark." The Master's Program has proven to be both rewarding to the individuals and highly rewarding to the sponsoring companies and organizations. Companies have saved millions of dollars through the team-based process improvement activities that have resulted from the learning and application of the students as a required part of their graduate study. The faculty are highly skilled and experienced, and the courses are uniquely designed. For more information, call 1-800-838-2580.